IN PURSUIT
OF THE PRIZE

Finding God in
the Great Outdoors

In Pursuit of the Prize

Copyright © 1998 by Jim Grassi
Published by Harvest House Publishers
Eugene, Oregon 97402

Library of Congress Cataloging-in-Publication Data
  Grassi, James E., 1943-
  In pursuit of the prize / Jim Grassi.
    p. cm.
    ISBN 1-56507-942-6
    1. Hunting–Religious aspects–Christianity.   2. Fishing–Religious aspects–Christianity.   3. Men–Religous life.   4. Hunters–Prayer-books and devotions–English.   5. Fishers–Prayer-books and devotions–English.   6. Men–Prayer-books and devotions–English. I. Title.
  BV4597.4.G73 1998
  242 '.68–dc21   98-14137
                                                      CIP

Design and Production by:
Koechel Peterson & Associates, Minneapolis, MN

The author wishes to thank Logos Research Systems for the use of their new software program that enabled him to efficiently research numerous Bible references.

Printed in Hong Kong.

98 99 00 01 02 03 04 05 06 07 /IM/ 10 9 8 7 6 5 4 3 2

Dedicated with deep appreciation
to all the men and women
who have inspired, directed,
and volunteered to work
with these outdoor ministries:

CHRISTIAN BOWHUNTERS OF AMERICA

CHRISTIAN DEER HUNTERS ASSOCIATION

CHRISTIAN SPORTSMAN'S FELLOWSHIP

FELLOWSHIP OF CHRISTIAN ANGLERS SOCIETY

FISHERS OF MEN

GOD'S GREAT OUTDOORS

LET'S GO FISHING FAMILY MINISTRIES

MY FATHER'S WORLD VIDEO MINISTRIES

And…
To the future generation of sportsmen,
especially my grandchildren
Dana Rose and Tyler Thomas Grassi

ACKNOWLEDGMENTS

I truly appreciate the support and encouragement I received on this project from countless individuals. As with the first-century church, ministry works best when teamwork is involved. First Corinthians 12 clearly identifies the benefits of cooperation and partnership while doing God's business. This project is a testimony to the comradeship in ministry.

The privilege of leading a dynamic work like Let's Go Fishing Ministries while tending to speaking engagements and developing this book had its challenges. I especially appreciate our committed board, staff, Proteam, volunteers, and supporters for their assistance and provisions during these engaging times. I wish to praise C.J. Addis and Craig Lee for being my partners in ministry and utilizing their spiritual gifts to the glory of God. My understanding wife, Louise, was willing to sacrifice some of our personal time so that this project could be undertaken—thank you.

To those special friends who provided illustrations for these devotionals, I wish to extend my heartfelt love and appreciation. Gerry Caillouet and Dr. Tom Rakow are two worthy outdoorsmen, without whom this project would have been much more difficult. Also, we appreciate the selected photographs from Tim Christie that added to the beauty of this book.

Finally, I cherish the friends and professionals at Harvest House Publishers. Their creative abilities and encouragement are key to this author's success. I'm reminded of what William Shakespeare said: "Thinking of friends and their worth is often enough to drive away an army of fears, regrets, and envies."

Thank you, God, for your beautiful creation and the ability to enjoy it!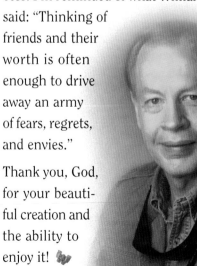

IN PURSUIT OF THE PRIZE

Finding God in the Great Outdoors

Harvest House Publishers
Eugene, Oregon 97402

Jim Grassi

FOREWORD

I really enjoy Jim Grassi's books. He knows how to glorify and enjoy God. There's a down-to-earth authenticity about his writing. Jim is a real person. What you see is what you get. And what you get is a man who loves God and sees His signature in nature.

Jim knows how to keep tight lines in fishing and in his writings. This book is filled with applications of the principles of good sportsmanship to live the Christian life. The author is a superb story-teller. He paints vivid word pictures with "you are there" clarity.

This devotional book with its stunning wildlife photographs by Tim Christie and Jim Grassi will find its way into the knapsack of any lover of fishing and hunting. It will bring inspiration and give fresh courage for living life to the fullest. The anecdotes are impelling, and the quotes are uplifting.

Here's an entertaining book that will make you laugh and cry, think and pray. You'll get to know God better and recapture the awe and wonder of enjoying the outdoors.

You are about to begin a wonderful adventure with one of God's very special people. You'll find that the pursuit of the prize is itself a truly great prize.

– Dr. Lloyd J. Ogilvie, *U.S. Senate Chaplain*

INTRODUCTION

W hether you are scanning the lake bottom for a trophy bass, stalking a great bull elk, or casting to a quiet pool, there is something exhilarating about the outdoor adventure. Many people will never experience the unique excitement of the hunt, the pure ecstasy of matching our human wits and skills against creatures of the wild. But the outdoorsman knows it well. The only part of sportsmanship that surpasses this thrill is the joy of surveying the beauty of God's great outdoors.

There is something almost mystical about a true wilderness adventure. Surrounded by the beauty of nature you feel more alive, more attuned to God. Your heart is filled with gratitude and with awe for One who could have created all the wonders that surround you. It puts you in a state of mind receptive to the deepest truths about life.

You also find yourself identifying with the struggles and challenges that confronted our forefathers when they settled in this beautiful country. And you quickly see the need to learn the skills and adaptations that are necessary to earn the distinguished title, "woodsman."

It is clear that others share my enthusiasm for these outdoor sports. There are more than 69 million outdoorsmen in the United States and no shortage of how-to books, videos, clinics, and instructors to teach you how to improve your skills. But when you boil down all the teaching and instruction, it can be summed up in a few simple truths. Qualities such as commitment, patience, perseverance, and willingness to apply new principles as you learn them are all key to becoming a skilled *outdoorsman*.

Similarly, if you pay attention to the innumerable books, videos, speakers, and conferences that offer to teach you how to be a better Christian disciple, you'll find that there are a handful of key traits that stand out above the others. Strangely enough, they are the same ones necessary to the outdoorsman: commitment, patience, perseverance, and the willingness to apply new principles as you learn them.

These parallels should not surprise us. Jesus understood the passions and pursuits of the outdoorsman, for in many ways, He was one Himself. He was a practical man who cared for the common adventurer. When it came to choosing His twelve apostles, His most trusted assistants, He largely chose fishermen. He called these outdoorsmen to leave their musty nets and smelly fish to catch the vision of His ministry. And when Jesus taught, He often chose anecdotes, metaphors, and stories that evoked the outdoors. He captured the imagination of the men and women who would change the world by pointing them toward the greatest adventure of all: a life as fishers of men and hunters of God's heart.

One of the joys of fishing and hunting is to be able to sit around the campfire and swap stories of your successes and failures—the deer you finally bagged after tracking it over long miles or the "big one that got away" during your fishing expedition. Our character is tested any time we are faced with new encounters and experiences. And when others join us in these adventures, a special bonding occurs. We recognize the value of trust, integrity, friendship, teamwork, wisdom, and respect for God's creation. We also learn something about ourselves, about our foolishness and failures as well as our extraordinary potential. No one leaves the wilderness the same person he was when he entered. He is changed mentally, physically, and spiritually. I can personally testify to that.

Tucked away in the annals of fishing and hunting are many stories that have taught the participants important lessons about life and living. In this book I will share some of my stories and those of my friends, and what I learned from my experiences in the wilds. I hope to inspire, encourage, and uplift you with the unfailing power of hope. May you grow in your desire to pursue not only the great outdoor adventure, but also to pursue the One who created everything we enjoy.

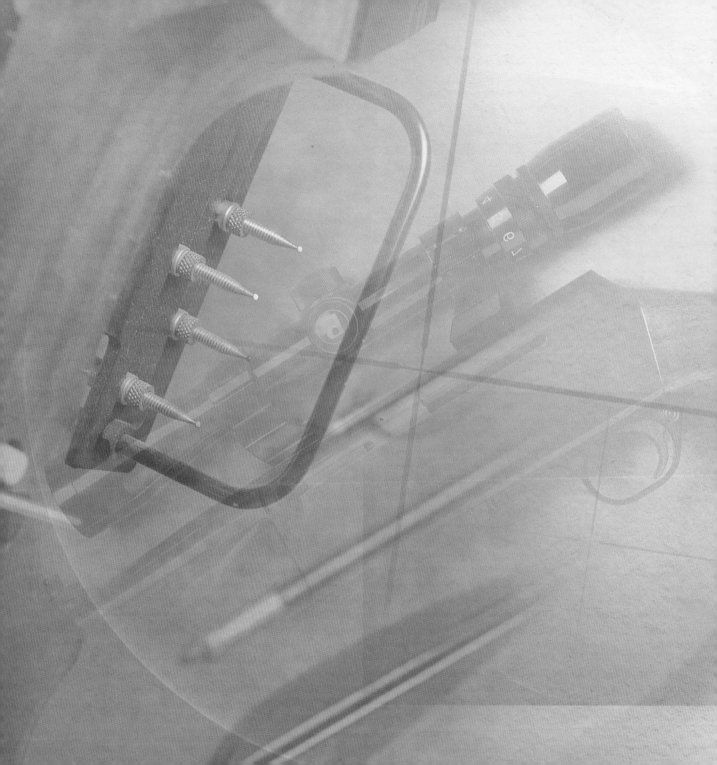

SET YOUR SIGHTS

READ: PSALM 27:4

Any marksman will tell you that you'll never hit your target if your aim is off. When you fire a rifle, you don't just point and shoot. You must carefully calculate the distance, hold the rifle very still, and, looking through your site, focus your attention upon the target. It is similar with archery. You must have a steady aim and site in on the target you want to hit.

If you don't keep the target in sight, your bullets and arrows are unlikely to find their mark. They will litter the ground around the target without actually ever hitting it.

It is the same for us in our Christian lives. We can expend all kinds of energy, but if we are not sited in on the target, we will always miss our goals. Throughout Scripture we see evidence of people who neglected to set their sights properly. Discouragement, anguish, failure, and defeat were the inevitable results of their improper focus. We will never reach our goals in the Christian life unless we focus on Jesus.

The apostle Peter learned this important lesson the hard way. In Matthew 14:22-33, we read the story of how the disciples were crossing the Sea of Galilee when a storm arose suddenly and put their little boat at risk. The wind came up and the boat rocked up and down on the furious waves. It was then that they caught sight of a ghostly personage walking to them across the water. Now Peter was a fisherman, so he knew that this water was deep and that it would not support the weight of a human body. After all, he had fished on this lake many times before. Then it dawned on him who this "ghost" was. It was Jesus Himself. "Take courage!" Jesus said, "It is I. Don't be afraid."

Now Peter, like most of us, could be a pretty impulsive guy. He was so impressed with the miracle that he blurted out, "Lord, if it is you, tell me to come to you on the water."

> Let your eyes look straight ahead, fix your gaze directly before you.
> PROVERBS 4:25

Jesus simply answered, "Come."

Fixing his sights upon the Lord, Peter stepped over the side of the boat and began to walk toward Jesus. But then he realized what he was doing and became frightened. As he began to take his eyes off of Jesus, Peter began to lose his footing. "When he saw the wind, he was afraid and, beginning to sink, cried out, 'Lord, save me!'" (Matthew 14:30). Peter is a perfect example of how we often act during times of crisis. When we take our gaze off the Lord, we will sink just as Peter did. But as long as we keep our attention on the Lord Jesus Christ, He will sustain us and help us through troubled times. To mature in our faith, we must stay focused on Him. He should be the target toward which our heart is aimed.

What difficulty are you experiencing? Are you keeping your focus centered on God's promises? For God is faithful, and He will not forsake you. He promises to help you through all the rough seas of life. But you must keep your sights upon Him.

A MIDNIGHT MOUNTAIN DESCENT

READ: PSALM 62:1

It's not every day that I make the news, but it happened during a recent hunting expedition in New Zealand. Sitting at a table, sipping a cup of hot coffee while I watched the sunrise through the open window, I opened the Christchurch morning newspaper only to find an article entitled "Copter Missing Over N. Canty." I had a hard time swallowing my gulp of coffee when I realized that this news item was about my ordeal of the night before.

I guess the blame for our predicament has to lie with me. We were hunting the Alpine Mountains of New Zealand for elusive mountain goats known as tahrs. To find them, you have to be willing to go deep into treacherous terrain, and a helicopter is the best option. Late in the day, when our pilot set the copter down on top of a mountain to adjust some equipment, I made my mistake. In adjusting my gear, my rifle barrel inadvertently rose into the path of the rotor blade. Not only did it make a terrible sound, but the dent that it left rendered the craft unfit to fly.

What were we to do? The moonless night, with its freezing temperatures, loomed before us. We sent out a signal with the transponder to let anyone able to pick up the signal know that we were in a desperate situation, but our guide had little hope of a quick rescue. Instead, we would have to make our way 4000 to 5000 feet down the mountain on foot to reach the valley floor. Our guide knew of an abandoned hunter's hut some three or four miles north of our descent point where we could find shelter from the bitter night air. But would we be able to see well enough to navigate our way around the steep cliffs that posed such a hazard?

> Let him have all your worries and cares, for he is always thinking about you and watching everything that concerns you.
> 1 PETER 5:7 TLB

My fully-loaded utility belt had always drawn jokes from my sporting companions. But not on this night. My ammunition, knives, sharpeners, survival kit, two power bars, a solar blanket and two small pen-lights were just about all we had. And none of us was dressed for the difficult descent which lay before us.

I knew, as I had known so many times before, that it would take God's help to bring us through. We prayed for His guidance and direction. Then, with limited light, we began to climb down the face of the mountain. It was slow and difficult work. Once we passed the dangerous cliffs, we still had to endure thick brush that scratched us, tangled in our clothing, and buffeted our bodies with each step. It didn't help that I had eaten very little that day due to an upset stomach, so I quickly grew more and more fatigued. On three separate occasions I had to sit down and evaluate whether I could go on. It would have been so easy to give up. But I was buoyed by my faith in Jesus and the encouragement and wisdom of my guide, Phil Wilson; the pilot, Phil Robinson; and my hunting partner, Jerry Ringer.

About 11 p.m. the temperature fell below freezing, but we persevered and I found myself able to draw on strength that was not my own. Cold and frightened, we finally reached the hunter's hut and started a fire to dry out our clothing. At about 1:30 a.m. we heard the welcome sound of a helicopter, and peering out the window into the darkness of the night, we could see the searchlights of a rescue craft. The Christchurch Garden City Rescue Crew had flown in the darkness through jagged mountains to search for our party.

Warming my hands over my coffee cup the next morning, I set aside my newspaper and thought about the ordeal I had been through. I thought about how the peril of my situation paralleled the peril of my life before I had recognized God's love and grace. I was truly in a hopeless situation until God reached out His hand to me. And ever since, I have experienced His divine touch in times of weariness, danger, and need. Like that rescue crew, He has flown into the darkness of my life to bring me out of the gravest situations. I owe everything to His mercy.

He is the One who sustains us during those times when we want to quit. He guides us when we have lost our way on the paths of life. And He is ready to help you just as He helped me that cold, dark night on the mountain. You can bring your prayers before Him knowing that He is able to rescue even the weariest.

A SPORTMAN'S BEST ASSET

READ: GALATIANS 6:10

For several years two Northern California fishermen were considered to be one of the very top teams in professional bass fishing. Dale Black and Rick Haley usually picked up a nice check at the end of every competition. What was their secret? Well, partly it was because they were talented fishermen. They knew their equipment and how to put it to the best use, and they had an exhaustive understanding of bass and their habits. But I think their secret went beyond that.

I have had the privilege of fishing with this team on a number of occasions. And while they have very good skills and knowledge, their most valuable asset is the way they encourage each other. They fish together in harmony, as a true team. They use every opportunity to uplift and support one another. Words of affirmation and encouragement flow freely from their lips. The dictionary tells us that to encourage is "to inspire with courage, spirit, or hope; to give help." These two men show this quality in action and success while pursuing their favorite sport.

In our lives we sometimes need this same kind of encouragement to keep going. Life can be very difficult, and its challenges can sometimes seem overwhelming. When we aren't at the top of our game, it is easy to find those who doubt us and are quick to criticize. But what we need is an encourager to come alongside us and keep our spirits up. And it is not only when we are down that we need encouragement. Even when things are going well, it is important for us to hear the positive affirmation that lets us know we are cared for and that someone believes in us and our abilities.

In His relationship with the disciples, Jesus proved to be a great encourager. We see this especially in the way He dealt with Peter. Although He sometimes had to call Peter to task for his foolishness and presumption, Jesus was quick to let Peter know how much potential He saw in this rough-hewn fisherman. In fact, Jesus proclaimed Peter the "rock" or foundation for the early church. And from the encouragement he received from the Lord, Peter found the strength to overcome his mistakes and serve God wholeheartedly.

Can we learn to follow the example that Jesus left for us? We are called to uplift one another, to encourage our families, our friends, and our co-workers. It is amazing how much a little word of encouragement and appreciation can accomplish. Are there people in your life who need to hear a word of encouragement from you? Maybe a son or daughter? Your wife? A fishing buddy? Why not follow the example of Jesus and of my friends Dale and Rick. Words of encouragement build strong relationships.

> I tell you that you are Peter,
> and on this rock
> I will build my church.
> MATTHEW 16:18

THE WHITEWATER YEARS

READ: DEUTERONOMY 6

Next to my relationship with God, there is nothing more important than my family, which now includes two daughters-in-law and two beautiful grandchildren. But as I look back, I remember how challenging it can be to raise children. Sometimes it can feel like we are rafting down a turbulent river, the swirling waves beyond our control.

This parallel looms large when I remember a trip I took with my son's Scout troop down the infamous North Fork of the American River.

Our troop arrived at the water's edge on a beautiful spring day. We slipped our raft into the placid current and slowly drifted downstream. As we floated, the guide provided instructions and discussed how we might handle various situations we might encounter. We paddled along, enjoying the beauty of God's creation and the fellowship with one another.

When we came to the first set of rapids, we were ready. We enjoyed the challenge of making our way through them. The next few were equally enjoyable. It wasn't until midday that we began to tackle the class-five areas, notoriously named "Satan's Cesspool," "Triple Threat," and "Flower's Rock." Despite our sense of preparedness for these obstacles, once we entered them we learned that navigating the whitewater was not the same as navigating the simple rapids. At times it was all we could do to hang on so that we wouldn't be thrown out of the boat. Paddling was out of the question!

This is a lot like the experience of parenting. The wind currents of the early years are usually pretty calm and enjoyable. We make plans, read books, and decide that being a parent is like a breezy day on a calm current. Then come the turbulent teenage years.

For some parents these times can seem like an eternity and feel like an experience far worse than any whitewater trip! It's true—in rafting and in parenting—there are times when all you can do is just hang on. I have to admit, we were pretty blessed as both our boys had very even dispositions. But I can remember sitting with friends who opened up

their hearts about the pain they were experiencing. Parenting teenagers seemed to be the ultimate test.

It helps to remember that you are not alone in the parenting task. Many support systems are in place to encourage you: family, church, good friends. They can help you through these trying times. It also helps to remember some wise advice: "Don't feel totally, personally, irrevocably, eternally responsible for everything. That's My job" –God.

Though you can't take God's role on yourself, there are some things you can do to make your job easier. I'd like to share five basic ingredients I have discovered that seem to be characteristic of the strongest families:

1. APPRECIATION. We all need to give and receive words of gratitude. A positive and supportive environment is a must if we are to develop our God-given talents and gifts. As Paul wrote, "Encourage one another and build each other up" (1 Thessalonians 5:11).

2. COMMUNICATION. We must keep the channels of communication open if we do not want to lose touch with our children. When did you last have a serious talk with your children about their lives and concerns?

3. TIME. In our day we have allowed the tyranny of the urgent to determine our schedules and the destiny of our families. We must slow down, sort out our priorities, and give our children the time they need with us. The family that plays together stays together.

4. COMMITMENT. In Scripture we find this wonderful promise regarding commitment: "Let us not lose heart in doing good, for in due time we shall reap if we do not grow weary" (Galatians 6:9 NASB). We are assured a good result if we are steadfast.

5. SPIRITUAL WELLNESS. Families that put God at the center of their lives are better able to weather life's storms. If you emphasize spiritual health and maintenance–especially by example– your family will experience the blessing of being in God's perfect will.

> He and all his family were
> devout and God-fearing;
> he gave generously to those in
> need and prayed to God regularly.
> ACTS 10:2

And always remember, in life as in rafting trips, the whitewater *will* pass.

LIONS, TIGERS & THE ELUSIVE BULL MOOSE

READ: JAMES 1:2

Russell Thornberry, editor of *Buckmaster* magazine, used to make his living as an outfitter and guide in the Canadian province of Alberta. He has many great stories to tell that arise from his experiences there. One of my favorites bears repeating (no pun intended).

In late September 1974, Russell was hunting for the elusive bull moose with a client. As Russell and his client made their way through the black spruce muskeg, they started calling for the big bull moose. A sudden hush fell over the area and a strange feeling settled on the hunters. Quietly at first, then with growing intensity, a strange beating sound began to fill the woods. The hearts of the hunters began to beat wildly as well in anticipation of spotting a moose. Looking up, Russell saw some movement in the distance, and within minutes the brush all around the two woodsmen began to stir. They gripped their rifles tight, tensing in preparation.

But it was not a bull moose. It was a pack of wolves, appearing in a semicircle around the hunters. "The sound we heard had been the panting of the running wolves," remembers Russell. "It all happened so quickly that it seemed almost imaginary."

Once the wolves realized that the hunters were not the moose they had hoped to feast upon, they fled as quickly as they had appeared. Russell knew that this kind of thing happened from time to time, but his disappointed client was not so quick to forgive and forget. What happened two days later only confirmed his frustration with hunting.

As nightfall was approaching, Russell and his client were hiding in a pile of dead trees still trying to use their persistent calling to attract a moose. They snapped to attention when they heard cracking and popping right behind them. Knowing that a bull moose will sometimes tiptoe up on unsuspecting hunters who are calling, Russell smiled to himself. His client would finally get to see the much-anticipated moose.

Slowly they turned around to get a look at the intruder. But it was not the intruder they had expected. Instead of a trophy moose, they found themselves staring face-to-face with a huge black bear. Only six feet away, the bear reared up on its hind legs and the hunters screamed in horror. A shot into the air caused the bear to vanish and left the hunters, half-laughing and half-crying, dancing a jig of uncontrollable nervous tension.

This misadventure was the final straw for Russell's client. He refused to believe that these were unusual situations, not at all the norm. He gave up outdoorsmanship on the spot. Russell suspects that he never left the comfort of his big city apartment again!

We all experience surprise encounters with the unexpected and the unwanted. Just because you are a Christian does not mean that you get to escape difficulties. Such an illusion is misleading and unbiblical. Troubles are sure to find us, even as they found our Savior during His time on this earth. But our confidence need not be shaken, as was that of Russell's client. We are not at the mercy of nature's mysteries, but of God's promises!

> The good man does not escape
> all troubles—he has them too.
> But the Lord helps him
> in each and every one.
> PSALM 34:19 TLB

Through faith in Jesus Christ, committed believers can count on the Lord being with them in every circumstance. He guarantees that He will undergird, inspire, motivate, and encourage us. He will give us His wisdom and comfort. Even when difficulties come, the Christian knows that God is in control. The "bears" and "wolves" we face in our lives will not defeat us!

The archer hunts not for meat, not for the trophy,
but for the sheer, pure joy of matching
wits and endurance
with that clever animal.

LAWRENCE R. KOLLER

TRACKING DEER AND THEIR MAKER

READ: JOHN 14:9

Successful deer hunters know the importance of looking for "the sign." When you are trying to locate a deer it makes a big difference if you can find a sign that tells you they were once there. If you know how to read the signs well, you might even get a good idea of how long it has been since the deer was in that location. A friend of mine once said, "Animals don't wear diapers and eat at McDonalds." Deer leave evidence of their presence. Wherever an animal walks, sleeps, feeds, mates, and plays, it will leave telltale signs. There may be a strong, heavy track; a matted weedy area that was used as a bed; a thrashed tree used for rubbing the velvet off antlers; cool, moist areas that the animal rolled in; or droppings and traces of urine flow. By analyzing these signs you can accurately predict the type of game, its gender, and its approximate size. All from the signs!

The Creator of the universe has also left His mark on our world. Paul reminds us that the signs of God's presence are so numerous that everyone knows something about Him. Everywhere around us He has left evidence of who He is, His power, His creativity, His wisdom, His love for us. The reality of His presence is revealed to every living thing by the awesome beauty and order of the world in which we live. Can you stand on a mountaintop taking in all the beauty that stretches out before you and honestly say it is all a result of chance? Or does it confirm to your heart and mind that it is the work of God?

The apostle Paul reminds us that we have no excuse if we fail to read the signs of God's reality: "For since the creation of the world God's invisible qualities–His eternal power and divine nature–have been clearly seen, being understood from what has been made, so that men are without excuse" (Romans 1:20). God has left His fingerprints all over His creation. And the signs of His presence testify to His magnificence.

> The heavens praise your wonders, O LORD, your faithfulness too, in the assembly of the holy ones.
> PSALM 89:5

Check out the signs. If you follow them you'll find the One worth pursuing with your whole heart.

NEVER GIVE UP!

READ: GALATIANS 6:9

At the peak of World War II, Sir Winston Churchill emboldened the troops with his succinct and now famous message: "Never give up!"

Not only is this good advice for an army under siege, it is also good advice for a hunter! Dwight Schuh, one of the most well-known bow hunters in the country and senior editor of *Bowhunter Magazine*, learned this lesson the hard way. Dwight is a great storyteller, and one of his favorite experiences to recount is when he was hunting Oregon's Blue Mountains on a blustery fall day.

> To those who by persistence in doing good seek glory, honor and immortality, he will give eternal life.
> ROMANS 2:7

He had been hunting for a while when he saw in the distance some plum bushes where a four-pointer was feeding. He lifted his spotting scope, and as he looked through it he thought about how nice it would be to see a really big deer. Suddenly, he says, "my daydreaming was interrupted when a massive set of antlers rose into my view from behind the first buck."

Dwight was flabbergasted. "The antlers reminded me of moose antlers, so grossly did they dwarf the other buck's rack. Never had I seen such an animal!" Dwight knew that at certain times of the year bucks will run together because of the protection it affords them against predators. He had been lucky enough to stumble upon such an occasion. He studied the animal and the landscape, plotting his strategy to bring down this massive buck.

He carefully began to stalk this trophy mule deer, patiently taking over an hour to circle around the canyon for a better shot. Crawling and sliding on his belly, he kept out of view. When a snow squall blew up, it changed the direction of the wind. As he finally was able to creep close to the patch of plum bushes where he thought the buck had been feeding, it appeared that the animal was gone.

Cold and frustrated, Dwight decided that the deer must have scented him and bailed out of the area. What a disappointment! Giving up, he waited out a snow flurry under a tree. Suddenly, a grouse jumped up on a rock about 15 feet away. Clucking and chirping, he seemed to be teasing the disappointed hunter. "I was freezing and hungry, and roast grouse seemed like just what the doctor would order to get over my case of the blues," he says. Convinced that the bucks were gone, Dwight shot a blunt-point arrow at his future dinner. But the arrow narrowly missed, clanging off a rock.

The noise of the arrow roused an explosion in the nearest plum bushes. Huge antlers erupted about 20 yards away as the two bucks sprang to their feet and

ran away from the area. He had already spent his arrow and did not have time to reload. Dwight had given up too soon. The largest mule deer he had ever seen was only 20 yards away from his position, but he had become impatient and had quit too early.

Like Dwight, many Christians give up too soon. Tired of waiting, we let go of our hopes and dreams, and miss the blessing God intended for us. We give up on a project because we run into a problem we can't easily solve. We let a relationship fall apart because it will take too much time and effort to repair it. Some even give up on life itself because it becomes too much of a chore.

What is God's counsel for those who feel like giving up? Hebrews 10:36 encourages us: "You need to persevere so that when you have done the will of God, you will receive what he has promised." In other words, never give up—never! Those who carry on for the long haul are those who will reap the prize.

Every fishing water has its secrets.
A river or a lake is not a dead thing.
It has beauty and wisdom and content.
And to yield up these mysteries,
it must be fished with more than hooks.

Zane Grey

SPIRITUAL STALKING

READ: JONAH 2:9

Two of the things that my friend Max and I have in common are a love for God and a passion for archery. We have often remarked to one another on the many similarities between being a bowhunter and being a Christian. We can also cite numerous Biblical analogies that point us to hunting, remembering that God used many great sportsmen to bring honor and glory to Him. There was David, who killed a lion and a bear with a sling, Nimrod, who was a "great hunter before God," Esau, described as a "skillful hunter," and King Solomon, who had scores of hunters bringing in "deer, gazelles, roebuck, and choice fowl."

One skill that every hunter must develop is that of stalking. As hunters we must learn to move swiftly and silently, listening intently as we weave our way through the forest. We slip around and creep next to game trails and feeding areas in order to find our target. We must carefully place each step, as the snap of a twig or the rustle of underbrush might alert our prey that we are nearby.

We should show no less concern for how we approach others with the truths of the spiritual life. By listening, absorbing, and discreetly stepping into relationships, we seek out tender hearts. The wise disciple is careful not to "scare away" the nonbeliever with the wrong approach. Instead, we practice spiritual discernment by recognizing the signs of an open heart and the impression of God's leading. Just as a hunter might, we wait for the right occasion to take our shot. Timing is critical. As in bow-hunting, we must wait for the precise moment to make our move. That means listening to God's leading.

> I press on toward the goal to win the prize for which God has called me heavenward in Christ Jesus.
> PHILIPPIANS 3:14

HUNTING ELK AND SOULS

READ: PROVERBS 25:11

Pick up almost any hunting magazine and you'll find many references to Dwight Schuh and Larry Jones. Their expertise has enriched the experience of numerous hunters. They have not only written fine articles, but also taken spectacular photographs and produced world-class hunting videos. One of their most famous videos is *Elk Fever*, which contains rare footage of a Pacific Northwest hunt and is filled with helpful advice for improving techniques for hunting bull elk with a bow and arrow.

One of the things that makes this video so enjoyable is seeing the cooperation and teamwork these men use to bring the elk within bow range. We watch while one archer calls and the other positions himself upwind from the animal. Then, when the bull gets close enough to one of the hunters, he fires his arrow. In addition to this hunting action, Dwight and Larry offer many practical tips for the hunter.

I was especially intrigued by the four "critical considerations" they point out for anyone involved in the sport of bowhunting. I couldn't help but think of how applicable they are to the strategies we need to keep in mind when we share the gospel with others.

First, the good hunter will thoroughly scout the area prior to the hunt, search out terrain that is elk-friendly, and look for signs of the animal's presence. In a similar manner, the one who shares the gospel should know all he can about the person with whom he wishes to share. We should scout out their interests, hobbies, friends, associations, vocation, and background. Until we demonstrate a genuine concern for the other person, we cannot expect to be able to discuss with him something as personal as his faith.

> All who
> win souls
> are wise.
> PROVERBS 11:30 TLB

Second, the good hunter will carefully study a good topographic map. He will try to identify key valleys, potential drainage areas, meadows, and north-facing slopes that could be hangouts for trophy bulls. The Christian who wants to share the gospel should study God's Word for guidance and examples. We should select and share passages that fit our friend's particular circumstances. For example, a fellow fisherman would probably be interested to know that 8 of Christ's 12 disciples were fisherman.

Third, the good hunter will learn about the elk and its habits. Being able to predict its reaction to your calls and intrusion will make you much more successful. The Christian who wants to share the gospel will learn to be people-savvy. Discussing issues of faith can be uncomfortable, so we must respect the beliefs of others and keep our conversations confidential. If you put yourself in your friend's shoes, you'll better understand his reactions.

Fourth, the good hunter will consider the part that weather will play in the hunt. While weather is something you can't control, you can utilize certain conditions to your benefit. Similarly, the discipler of men is dependent upon the Holy Spirit to prepare a person's heart and mind. Don't get ahead of the Spirit or you may find your efforts "rained out."

And remember, as exhilarating as it can be to hunt for elk, there is nothing more rewarding than being a hunter of men's souls.

THE CRUEL TRUTH ABOUT FISH AND FAIRNESS

READ: MATTHEW 20: 1-16

I think that some of the most joyous times we ever had as a family were those spent on a houseboat on California's beautiful Lake Shasta, just south of the Oregon border. We built lasting memories with our young sons during those vacations where we spent our time fishing, boating, and water-skiing. Some of the memories are of the fun we had. Others deal with important lessons our boys learned about life; for example, the painful truth that we must all learn sooner or later: Sometimes life is not fair.

> Of his fulness have we all received, and grace for grace. For the law was given by Moses, but grace and truth came by Jesus Christ
> JOHN 1:16,17 KJV

My wife and I were blessed with twin sons, Dan and Tom, who have learned to love God's creation with the same kind of passion as their father. At the early age of three they caught the fishing bug. The boys were equally gifted in natural ability and quickly became proficient in the sport. By the age of eleven they were using bait and casting reels with the kind of dexterity usually reserved for veterans of the sport. But though they were equally talented, they soon learned that the fish did not bite with fair and equal consideration. One boy would find himself reeling in fish after fish, proudly holding them up for all to see, while the other got "skunked." Not a bite, not a nibble. Sometimes we would keep fishing for several extra hours, just trying to equal the score between these competitive boys!

On one "unfair" fishing expedition, one of my sons was having a particularly frustrating day. Finally, he looked up at me with tears welling in his eyes and said, "Daddy, when is it going to be my turn?" But in fishing it is not always as simple as waiting for our turn. We can bestow equal amounts of praise and reward on our children, but the fish are not so kind! When we'd bring our catch back into the dock, the attendants and spectators were quick to praise whoever brought in the biggest stringer. Dan and Tom saw that the world's view of success is usually based only on end results.

Sometimes that is not fair. Sometimes life, like fishing, isn't fair.

But would we really want it to be? Would we really want to get exactly what we deserve? Or should we be thankful that God's grace overcomes our unworthiness, that He offers us more than we deserve? Isn't our human scale of values inadequate when it comes to questions of fairness?

In the twentieth chapter of Matthew, Jesus taught His disciples an important parable about God's view of fairness. It demonstrated to them the even handedness and equality of God's love and grace. The parable begins, "For the kingdom of heaven is like a landowner who went out early in the morning to hire men to work in his vineyard." As the story unfolds we see the landowner hiring people throughout the day. The last man is hired with only

one hour left to work, but he is paid the same as those who worked all day. "Unfair!" grumble many of the workers who had labored all day long in the hot sun. "These men who were hired last worked only one hour, and you have made them equal to us who have borne the burden of the work and the heat of the day" (verse 12).

But the landowner's response shows how God looks beyond mere fairness. "Friend, I am not being unfair to you. Didn't you agree to work for a denarius? Take your pay and go. I want to give the man who was hired last the same as I gave you. Don't I have the right to do what I want with my own money? Or are you envious because I am generous?" (Matthew 20:13-15).

When you really consider it, aren't you glad that God looks beyond fairness? That our Savior doesn't measure our worthiness for the kingdom by how long we have been Christians, how often we go to church, how many prayers we offer up to God, or how many good deeds we have done? While these things are important to our spiritual development, Jesus tells us in this parable that we are all equally forgiven and blessed because of *His* actions, *His* generosity. We all enter heaven on an equal footing if we put our trust in Christ.

Experience is indeed the best teacher.
Such is deer hunting.
Every time I walk into the woods,
I learn something new.

STEVE CHAPMAN

NATURE BY NIGHT

READ: EPHESIANS 5:20

L arry Hemphill, a.k.a. "Lunker Lar," is well-known in Northern California as the "Night Stalker," a nickname he earned because he enjoys fishing at night. Few things bring him as much pleasure as launching his boat onto the lake in the darkness of a moonlit night and fishing into the early hours of the next day. He has learned by experience that many of the larger bass will freely roam the shallow water once the sun has set and there is less activity on the surface of the water.

> How many are your works, O Lord! In wisdom you made them all; the earth is full of your creatures.
> PSALM 104:24

Several years ago, Lunker Lar took San Francisco Giants' manager Dusty Baker and a couple of his friends on one of his moonlight excursions to Clear Lake. Shortly after dusk, Dusty gave a yell and leaned back on his seven-foot rod as a spunky five-pound bass came charging out of the water. With a flick of its head, the bass pulled the black plastic worm off the hook and threw it into Dusty's lap. Of course, the boat erupted in howls of laughter. Once everyone had recovered from the hilarity of the situation, Larry reminded Dusty that a strong hook set is crucial to successful bass fishing!

As the night passed, everyone grew quieter and more contemplative. With the moon shining on the calm lake, conversation centered on the beauty of the stars, the awesomeness of the heavens, and the wonder of God's great creation. Because it is so still in the darkness, night fishing brings sounds to your ears that you might otherwise fail to notice. And with this stillness comes a sense of peace. As anyone who has experienced the evening glories of God's universe will acknowledge, "The heavens declare the glory of God; the skies proclaim the work of his hands" (Psalm 19:1).

Still pondering all the beauty and serenity of the evening, Dusty suddenly felt a tug on his rod. This time he swung back so hard we thought he was going to throw himself out of the boat. "You're not going to get away from me this time!" he hollered. The powerful six-pounder jumped out of the water, shaking its silver-brown body in the moonlight. Dusty planted the hook and brought the trophy fish aboard as high-fives flew liberally around the boat. It was the perfect way to cap an evening of contemplating the magnitude of God's handiwork.

When was the last time you thanked God for His many blessings and the wonder of His creation? Have you thanked Him for this glorious day and the health you have to enjoy the planet He made? We need to express our appreciation for the entire spectrum of nature: the creatures, trees, rocks, streams, leaves, all the vast wonder of His creation. We need to stop in the stillness and give Him glory.

A PERFECT COMPASS

READ: ROMANS 8:9

Getting lost is never fun. It can be very disconcerting to be making your way through the woods only to realize that you have lost your way, that you no longer know where you are. For a fisherman or a hunter, being able to locate your exact position or the areas fish and wildlife frequent is a critical necessity. At times it could even be a matter of life and death. For years sportsmen have utilized a pocket compass to orient themselves. It is often less than ideal, as it requires some interpretation and can be affected by other metal objects.

But most sportsmen had to make do, as the really accurate equipment was prohibitively expensive and often too bulky for any portable use.

In the early 1990s, however, the Humminbird Corporation changed all this by creating a portable global positioning system (GPS) that utilized commercial satellite receivers to help the sportsman accurately define his coordinates anywhere in the world. Quickly the market became saturated by GPS units of every size, shape, and price. There are now at least 24 satellites that broadcast radio signals from 12,000 miles above the earth to aid the outdoorsman, and the base maps which are built into some systems cover all major roads and cities. They can guide you to any location. As an advertisement from one manufacturer boasted, "The world is a big place, but finding yourself in a big world isn't a problem anymore thanks to GPS."

Receive
the
Holy Spirit.
JOHN 20:22

There is a guidance system available to the believer that is even more powerful than GPS. It may not necessarily guide you out of the forest when you are lost, but it guides you out of the spiritual darkness of a fallen world.

Those who have accepted Jesus Christ as their personal Savior have been given an internal guidance system. He is known as the Holy Spirit, and His mission is to guide us into truth.

This guidance system doesn't run out of batteries and is not affected by ozone layers or sunspots. It is a gift of God that will help guide you when you are lost, comfort you when you are lonely, inspire you when the going gets tough, convict you when your course is set for destruction, and direct you into God's path for your life. This guidance system cannot be purchased at any price, for God gives it freely to those who give their hearts to His Son.

FISH AREN'T THE ONLY THING THAT'S SLIPPERY

READ: EXODUS 15:2

I have to admit that I was very eager to begin our day fishing on a remote tributary of the Motu River in New Zealand. A year earlier I had visited the same area and fished this same pristine creek. Within a dozen casts I had caught and released a beautiful nine-pound German Brown trout. I was hoping that today we might run into some of his cousins.

But the dry algae and moss on the rocks was a discouraging sign; this creek had been dropping fast during the past few weeks. Each cast into the crystal-clear water produced only disappointment. The fluctuating water level was working with the recent full moon to put the fish off biting.

Deciding that this particular area was not going to be very fruitful today, my partners Mark and Gary joined me in a journey downstream. Hopping from rock to rock we worked our way down the river, stopping to fish the larger pools.

We had been doing this for some time when I decided to move on again. The nice little riffle I'd been working hadn't produced anything, so I began a sneak move toward the next pool. But I hadn't counted on the slipperiness of the rock I stepped onto. Despite a wading staff and some good shoes, my wet soles had greased the dried moss to the point that it was hazardous. My foot slipped out from under me, my body lunged forward, and my knee hit a jagged rock that rose out of the water. The hot, piercing pain that shot up

my leg was so overwhelming that I failed to notice right away that I had also damaged my hand, my wrist, and my equipment.

Within seconds Mark and Gary were at my side, but the agony was so intense that I couldn't speak or move my leg for a good five minutes. Soon the swelling and pain confirmed I was finished for the day. My partners knew they would have to get me some help, so they built me a fire, gave me some granola bars, and headed back for camp. Once I was alone, the minutes seemed like hours and the hours like days. But I had no choice but to wait.

It was a long wait. But as I waited, my comfort was in knowing that God was in control. Like King David I had to remind myself to "wait on the Lord: be of good courage, and he shall strengthen thine heart" (Psalm 27:14 KJV). Waiting is difficult, but that is often what God calls us to do. The waiting time can become a time of building a closer relationship with Him.

Alongside the river the hours passed slowly. Every hour I hobbled down to the frigid water to bathe my wounded knee. And just as the water soothed my leg, so prayer soothed my spirit. A heart-to-heart conversation with the Almighty has a way of helping us put the circumstances of our lives into balance. By the time my friends returned, I had great peace about what I was going through.

The wound was not too serious. Within a few days I was once again walking the banks of another quiet New Zealand stream. But I was also thinking about all the slippery rocks we face in our lives and the lesson I'd learned about waiting upon God to strengthen us in the hard times of our lives.

> They that wait upon the Lord shall renew their strength.
> ISAIAH 40:31 KJV

WHAT IS A FISHERMAN?

READ: LUKE 5

An old joke suggests that a fisherman is a jerk on one end of the line waiting for a jerk on the other end. I suppose that could be true of some anglers, but I'd like to suggest a better definition: The true fisherman is a committed sportsman who pursues his prey with dedication and zeal.

When I stop to consider it, I am amazed by the number of correlations that exist between the modern fisherman and those first-century disciples whom Jesus called to be "fishers of men." I believe it was no coincidence that Jesus picked eight fishermen to be among His twelve disciples. As dedicated fishermen, they had just the kind of qualities that Jesus was looking for in His followers.

The successful sportsman holds much in common with the successful disciple. When we examine what makes a good fisherman, we can see a

> As Jesus was walking beside the Sea of Galilee, he saw two brothers, Simon called Peter and his brother Andrew. They were casting a net into the lake, for they were fishermen. "Come, follow me," Jesus said, "and I will make you fishers of men." At once they left their nets and followed him.
> MATTHEW 4:18-20

powerful example of what it means to be a "fisher of men." Let's reflect on some of the similarities.

1 FISHERMEN ARE SUCH A PASSIONATE, PERSISTENT BREED THAT THEY ARE FREQUENTLY MISUNDERSTOOD BY OUTSIDERS. They come from all walks of life and spend countless hours preparing, analyzing, evaluating, and pursuing their beloved sport. Likewise, fishers of men don't lend themselves to a single ecclesiastical job description. Instead, they come from every profession, income level, culture, and background. They too are zealous in their pursuit of what they are called to: "catching others for Christ" (see Matthew 4:19).

2 FISHERMEN ARE INQUISITIVE BY NATURE. They seek adventure and exploration, never content with the routine or the mundane. Similarly, a fisher of men is one who is willing to go anywhere or do anything for the gospel, always ready to meet new people and new challenges in fulfilling Christ's mission.

3 FISHERMEN ARE OPTIMISTIC BY NATURE. They'll not easily give up because they earnestly believe that the very next cast may

produce a fish, even if they have had no luck the whole day long. Likewise, the fisher of men is one who lives by faith, not by sight (2 Corinthians 5:7), trusting God to bring good results from their efforts (and even from their failures!). They keep working. They keep trying.

4 FISHERMEN WORK HARD TO DEVELOP THEIR NEEDED SKILLS AND KNOWLEDGE. They study the habits and habitats of fish and practice their casting skills with determination. They take the necessary time to prepare in advance for their fishing adventure. In the same way, the fishers of men devote themselves to prayer and study to prepare themselves to understand God's Word and the world around them. They don't want to venture out unprepared.

5 FISHERMEN TAKE RISKS AND OVERCOME THE OBSTACLES PLACED BEFORE THEM. Fishing is not always easy or risk free. That doesn't stop the true fisherman. Neither do such risks and obstacles stop the fisher of men. The disciple is willing to risk fishing deeper waters for the bountiful harvest God has prepared (Luke 5).

6 FISHERMEN LOVE TO SHARE THE JOY OF THEIR CHOSEN PURSUIT. They are always willing to bend your ear with "fish stories." Similarly, the fisher of men is eager to share with others what Christ has done in his life.

Are you a true fisherman when it comes to catching souls for God's kingdom?

STICKY TRIGGER FINGER

READ: MATTHEW 28

One of the outdoorsmen I most admire is Gerry Cauillouet, host of *God's Great Outdoors*. Gerry is a gifted communicator and woodsman who has, through the years, been a great encouragement to many Christian sportsmen. Gerry is a man who pays attention to the lessons he learns from his favorite sport, hunting.

Some years ago, Gerry was shotgun-hunting an old logging road cut alongside a ridge in the hills of southeast Ohio. This was an area he had hunted many times, so he knew it like the back of his hand. The day was perfect for still-hunting. The leaves were wet, the sky was overcast with an occasional light flurry of snow, and there were deer signs all around him. He figured that this would be his day to take a nice trophy buck.

About midday Gerry was halfway up the road when a nice eight-point buck descended from the ridgetop, heading toward an old scrape area where the road and the ridge met. "The buck stopped just before dropping onto the flat," Gerry reports. "I prepared to shoot just as soon as he came into my shotgun range."

But when the buck moved into range, Gerry didn't pull the trigger. "It wasn't buck fever or a sudden feeling of guilt," he remembers. "I really can't explain why I didn't drop the animal when I had the chance." Shifting position to close the gap even more, Gerry slowly approached the deer by quietly crossing a small depression. This time the buck turned broadside and presented the perfect shot. Gerry raised his gun to fire, but again he hesitated. The wind began to swirl and the buck winded him. Gerry was spotted. "Emotion rushed upon me and screamed *Shoot*!" he says, "but I still could not pull the trigger." The animal spun and headed across the overgrown logging trail as Gerry placed his sights on the chest of the runaway critter. He finally squeezed off a shot: boom! Unfortunately, the buck ran behind a poplar tree. The deer escaped unscathed.

He has often analyzed his unfortunate choices that day. "I kicked myself many times for blowing the opportunity," Gerry admits. "I often think how many times I could have taken that deer. I will probably never have another chance to take a trophy animal that close again."

Don't we all have a tendency to hesitate in the face of our opportunities? How many missed chances can you point to in your life? Opportunities to build a relationship, assist a disabled person, or encourage a child? What about the last time you could have shared your faith but didn't?

> You will receive power when the Holy Spirit comes on you; and you will be my witnesses… to the ends of the earth.
> ACTS 1:8

We must take advantage of the opportunities that present themselves. We should be bold to love others, to share the gospel with unbelievers, to reach out to someone in need. Next time you are in a situation where you can act for God, don't freeze up while you wait for another chance or a better opportunity. Pull the trigger on it!

THE MAMA BEAR

READ: HEBREWS 12

Photographers have been known to go to great lengths to get a good picture. But everyone has his limits. Even Tim Christie, the award-winning nature photographer. Tim takes some of the most beautiful photographs you will ever see, capturing the outdoors in a way that truly glorifies the Creator. In fact, a number of his wonderful images grace the pages of this book.

During one of his winter photographic safaris in Glacier Park, Tim noticed a few whitetail deer casually feeding along the roadway. Grabbing his camera and film, Tim quietly slid out of his truck and began shooting. As the deer continued to feed, they moved into the woods. Tim followed them. He was getting many great shots when, through his viewfinder, he noticed that one of the deer looked startled. Just as the deer turned and scampered off, Tim heard a branch snapping in the woods behind him.

He turned to see a large grizzly sow making her way toward him. While he momentarily considered what a marvelous opportunity this would be to take the bear's picture, he changed his mind when he noticed that she had two cubs with her. It was clear that this mama bear was in no mood for a casual photo shoot. She was doing what comes naturally to any mother—protecting her young.

Tim dropped the camera and scrambled up the nearest tree. The bear followed. The higher he climbed, the higher the bear climbed, snapping her jaws and growling like a wounded hound. As the bear closed the gap, she made a grab for Tim's foot. Tim remembers a moment of tug-of-war over who would end up with his leg. Then his shoe came loose from his foot. The bear lost her balance and tumbled from the tree, hitting the ground with a thud.

The mother bear roared with disappointment, but gave up after a few minutes and disappeared into the woods with her cubs. Tim waited in the tree for a full two hours before he finally climbed down and gathered up his camera and his shoe. He made his way back to the truck as quickly as possible.

We all face scary moments in our lives. They may not be a growling bear, but they can make us worried and concerned. They can cause us to want to give up. But when trials come, the Lord asks us to do two things: trust and endure. We need to believe that God will see us

through and that He will give us the strength we need. The writer of Hebrews reminds us of the hostility Jesus endured so that we could have hope. "Let us fix our eyes on Jesus, the author and perfecter of our faith, who for the joy set before him endured the cross, scorning its shame, and sat down at the right hand of the throne of God. Consider him who endured such opposition from sinful men, so that you will not grow weary and lose heart" (Hebrews 12:2,3).

Don't give in, don't give up, and don't look down! Even when trouble and danger pursue you like that mama bear, know that God will give you the strength to pull through.

Blessed is the man who perseveres under trial, because when he has stood the test, he will receive the crown of life that God has promised to those who love him."

JAMES 1:12

THE ATTITUDE OF A SURVIVOR

READ: NEHEMIAH 8:10

Sometimes a positive attitude can be a matter of life or death. Such is the case with the true story (recorded by Francie Baltazar-Schwartz) of a pheasant hunter named Dave. Dave was not only an avid pheasant hunter, he was also a man with an unflappable attitude toward life. He always seemed to be in a good mood, always speaking words of encouragement to others, always quick to try to motivate others to see life from his sunny perspective. When anyone asked him how he was doing, Dave would usually reply, "If I were any better, I would be twins!"

Because he was such an upbeat guy, all his friends loved to go hunting with him. Even the hunting dogs seemed to sense that there was something different about Dave! Fellow hunters who spent time around Dave sometimes grew curious about how he was able to maintain such a positive outlook. "I don't get it," one of his friends said to him once. "You can't be a positive person all the time. How do you do it?"

> I will rejoice in the Lord, I will rejoice in the God of my salvation.
> HABAKKUK 3:18 KJV

"Well," Dave replied, "it's all a matter of choice. Each morning I wake up and I say to myself, 'Dave, you have two choices today. You can choose to be in a good mood or you can choose to be in a bad mood.' I choose to be in a good mood. Each time something bad happens, I can choose to learn from it. Every time I hear people complaining, I can listen to their moans or I can point to the positive side of life. I choose the positive!"

The other hunter looked at Dave dubiously and suggested that it was not that easy. "Yes it is!" said Dave firmly. " Life is all about choices. When you cut away all the junk, every situation is a choice. You choose how you will react to situations. You choose how people will affect your mood. You choose whether you want to believe in the positive message of the Christian faith or follow the negativity of worldly thinking. The bottom line: It's your choice how you live your life."

Not long after this conversation, Dave had the opportunity to demonstrate the strength of his conviction. While pheasant hunting with another friend, they came upon a barbed wire fence they had to climb over. Dave leaned his loaded shotgun against the fence and carefully spread the wires to make space to climb through. Unfortunately, the shotgun was not steady, and it fell hard against a supporting pole, causing the shotgun to discharge. It all happened so fast that there was nothing Dave could do. He fell to the ground, his shirt covered in blood from the multiple pellets that had lodged in his chest.

Shot in a critical area and losing a lot of blood, Dave had to be rushed to the nearest trauma center. Still conscious, he noted the frantic attitude of the emergency room people as they evaluated whether or not he could survive surgery to repair the horrible wounds. One burly nurse asked him, "Are you allergic to anything?" Dave took a deep breath as the doctors awaited his answer. "Yes," he responded with a forced smile, "I'm allergic to these pellets!"

After the laughter died down in the emergency room, a quiet peace came over the operating team. Their whole attitude toward him seemed to change. They could see that he was not a quitter—that neither should they give up hope but should operate on him as though he were already a survivor! And he was. He came through the surgery with flying colors, largely due to his positive attitude.

Like Dave, we must make choices about how we will respond to the situations we encounter in our lives. If we are believers in Christ, we should respond like believers! If I was to paraphrase Ephesians 4:22,23, it would go something like this: "You were taught, with regard to your former way of life, to put off your old self [that harbors negativity and pessimism], which is being corrupted by its deceitful desires [of lust and greed]; to be made new in the [positive] attitude of your minds; and to put on the new self [as a believer in Christ], created to be like God in true righteousness and holiness."

Choose to think positive!

The most important thing for hunting
is not whether a new world-record whitetail is killed.
It's planting the seed so future generations can
experience the greatest outdoor experience there is:
hunting white-tailed deer
on crisp autumn mornings.

CHARLES J. ALSHEIMER

A LIFE GUIDE

READ: PSALM 119:11

Homer Circle has proven to be a valuable guide to fishermen everywhere. I think it would be hard to find anyone in the fishing industry who is more universally loved and appreciated than "Uncle" Homer. Long before fishing even existed as a professional sport, Homer was promoting it with warmth and enthusiasm. He has spent his adult life teaching people how to enjoy fishing more by improving their skills. He has been a sports editor, a tackle manufacturing executive, and an oft-featured writer for *Sports Afield* magazine. And he has always been a teacher, a mentor, and a guide.

Many folks got their first glimpse into the winsome personality of this fishing patriarch through the classic film *Big Mouth*. For this film, Homer joined forces with world-renowned videographer/producer Glen Lau. They spent thousands of hours filming underwater to reveal the secrets of how black bass acted in their natural habitat. They worked hard and dove deep to retrieve priceless footage of the fish. The result was a revelation to bass fishermen everywhere.

To discover how fish reacted to various presentations, Uncle Homer introduced a variety of lures as Glen's crew filmed how the fish responded.

Out of the hours of hard work came a great film and many new insights into bass fishing. The kind of study they did showed how one might become a better fisherman.

> Your word is a lamp to my feet and a light for my path.
> PSALM 119:105

Studying is important in any discipline. In the spiritual life, as in fishing, we need the insights we can glean from diligent study. Over the years I have learned that if you really want to know spiritual truths, you have to carefully study God's Word. And it's not as hard to read and understand as you might think. There are countless study Bibles and new translations of the Bible that will make it come to life for you.

In the pages of the Bible, you will find many stories about people who dealt with problems that are similar to those you and I face every day. You will find teachings that are relevant to what you are going through in your life right now. You will also find the insight and inspiration to grow in character and become the kind of person God wants you to be. In the Bible we have the guide we need to teach us the secrets of successful living.

THE PIED PIPER OF THE WOODS

READ: JOHN 3

The name Charlie Alsheimer is almost synony- mous with whitetail deer hunting. Through the two magazines he edits, *Deer and Deer Hunting* and *Whitetail Business*, he has been responsible for pointing many people to the joys of hunting. Besides his journalistic work, he has also headed a 200-acre facility for hunting research and spoken to countless hunters on the practices and habits of these animals.

> Seek first the kingdom of God and his righteousness, and all these things will be given to you as well.
>
> MATTHEW 6:33

Charlie has been responsible for a number of impor- tant breakthroughs in cataloging the habits of the whitetail deer. His theories have revolutionized the understanding of this species for countless hunters. Most of these important insights came about as the result of research he was able to conduct over an eight-year period on one particular deer, whom locals came to call "Charlie the Deer." (Sometimes they referred to him as Charlie II to differentiate him from Mr. Alsheimer). Charlie II came into Charlie's life as a result of God's faithfulness.

Having survived Vietnam and the rigors of a corpo- rate life, Charlie understood the stresses and trials of the "real world." When the unhealthy pressures of his high-stress job began to take their toll on Charlie and his family, he decided that enough was enough. In 1979 he took a giant leap of faith and quit his job in order to pursue his true passion in life: communicating the wonder of God as it is found in the outdoors. Charlie soon learned that it isn't easy to make a career of writing, but He sensed God's leading and trusted in Him to provide.

In 1987 Charlie was on an estate in upstate New York writing an article on whitetail deer and photo- graphing a few nice bucks who had been lured in by his corn bait. Finishing off the bait, the animals moved on, and Charlie slipped out of his blind to rebait the area. It was then that God brought the other "Charlie" into his life. As he moved toward the baited area the rattling of the corn in his coffee can drew the attention of a one-year-old buck who "came out of nowhere." This young animal seemed unafraid. As Charlie said, "It was as if God placed this deer in my life."

Charlie tossed corn to the young buck until the coffee can was empty. As a result of feeding the buck there seemed to be some sort of bonding. On several follow-up trips the same deer followed Charlie wherever he went. The sound of the corn rattling in the can was always enough to attract him.

Over the course of the next several years the two Charlies became very close. The deer allowed Charlie to photograph his eating habits, mating rituals, scraping exercises, fights with other bucks, and bedding areas. All kinds of valuable data about whitetail deer became available to Charlie because of the relationship they had forged. The resultant articles and photographs sold at a brisk pace, helping Charlie properly care for his family.

For eight years his relationship with

that buck provided Charlie with many valuable insights. When he finally died of natural causes, Charlie buried the majestic eight-point buck deep in the woods and thanked God for sending Charlie II into his life. He understood the important part that the deer had played in his career and was grateful that God had brought the two Charlies together.

God always knows what we need in our lives, better than we know ourselves. If we are faithful and trust in His direction, God will provide just what we need, whether it be a new job, financial help, or a fearless young buck named Charlie.

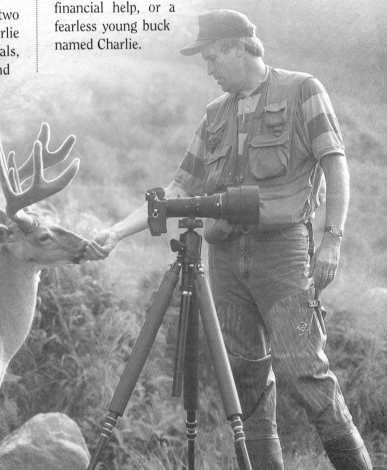

THE REAL FISHERMEN

THERE ARE VARIOUS TYPES OF FISHERMEN
DISCIPLES, ALL OF WHOM SEEM TO FALL INTO
ONE OF THE FOLLOWING CATEGORIES:

PHILOSOPHERS
Those who think about fishing.

SCHOLARS
Those who study fishing, but stay at home
and never actually see a lake or stream.

OBSERVERS
Those who stand on the shore and watch others fish.

PRETENDERS
Those who go through the motions but believe that
their equipment isn't really good enough to catch fish.

SKEPTICS
Those critical of the whole idea of fishing.

SPONSORS
Those who write a check to enable others to fish.

FREELOADERS, TICKS, AND PARASITES
Those who partake of the meal
after someone else has caught the fish.

FISHERMEN/DISCIPLES
Those who pursue the sport with passion and zeal.

THE STILLNESS OF THE HEART

READ: PSALM 127

Many skills must be developed in order to be a good hunter or fisherman. Some of these require a great deal of practice. Others demand diligent focus and concentration. Some forms of sportsmanship have skills which are specific to that sport alone. But one discipline is required in almost every outdoor sport: patient quietness.

Whether you are slip-hunting from tree to tree, sitting in a tree stand, or dunking bait in your favorite fishing hole, it is essential that you master the ability to be patient and quiet. The hunter or fisherman who becomes impatient or who makes excessive noise will rarely be successful.

In our fast-paced, instant-everything society, these sports offer a unique opportunity to quiet down, slow down, and take life at God's pace rather than our own. Fish and wildlife do not exhibit migraines, ulcers, heart attacks, hives, or other stress-related diseases. If undisturbed, they are rarely hurried or anxious. Through all my hunting and fishing expeditions I have learned that to be successful in the outdoors—and in life—we must slow down our pace. And we must listen—for the snap of a twig, the rustling in the underbrush, and the rise of a fish taking an insect from the surface are sounds that are key to our success.

Sportsmen know the wonderful tranquillity the outdoors provides. Through the rustling of the trees, chirping of the birds, and the sound of water rushing along over the rocks, we can hear God's quiet voice. On the other hand, it is difficult for us to hear Him speak to us through the noise and confusion of pagers, cell phones, faxes, voice mail, and crowded office buildings. If we want to hear the quiet communication of God we must slow down, be patient, and quiet down all the turmoil in our hearts and lives.

> Be still,
> and know
> that I
> am God.
> PSALM 46:10

When Jesus walked this earth, He never seemed to be in a hurry. He would frequently take time to get away from the crowds and be alone with the Father. From these times He received the inspiration and refreshment for His spirit that He needed to keep doing the work to which God had called Him. In fact, when the tired and weary disciples returned from their first ministry experience, Jesus gave them very simple directions: "Come away with me by yourselves to a quiet place and get some rest" (Mark 6:31). He offers the same invitation to us today!

THE JOYFUL LURE

READ: PHILIPPIANS 1:18-26

The engaging personality of tournament champion and television show host Jimmy Houston has won the hearts of many anglers. People think of him not only as a great fisherman, but also as a great man. Anyone who comes into contact with him is drawn to his positive attitude, an attitude which can best be described as infectious. Could it have been Jimmy that Samuel Shoemaker had in mind when he said, "The surest mark of a Christian is not faith, or even love, but joy." Jimmy Houston is a man whose life manifests joy.

But what is joy? Though it is a word used repeatedly in the Bible, I wonder if we have given much thought to what it really means. Joy, I want to suggest, is an attitude that is characterized by a feeling of deep satisfaction, pleasure, and fulfillment. It is the contentment and calmness that result from a strong and abiding faith in the power and grace of the Almighty. As such, it is a cornerstone for developing the kind of character that God wants to see in His children.

Joy is not dependent upon circumstances. We can have joy even in the midst of suffering and pain. Paul wrote his letter to the Philippians, sometimes known as "the epistle of joy," from a prison cell. Paul was able to encourage other believers to react to life as he was responding. "Rejoice in the Lord always!" he wrote, though he was probably in chains as he penned the words.

How can someone be joyful when things don't go the way they want them to? This is hard for us to understand because we tend to confuse joy with happiness. Happiness is dependent upon the circumstances of our life. We are happy when the job promotion comes, when our financial dreams come true, when our favorite team wins the crucial game and advances to a bowl berth. These are the things that make us happy. But our happiness is changeable. It depends on the weather, our mood, or whether we've had our morning coffee yet! This happiness lasts only until our next trial or failure occurs. Then unhappiness tends to set in.

But joy is something deeper and more lasting. It is based upon an eternal perspective, upon the knowledge that God is working in our lives and that He loves us deeply. With joy we can endure even the deepest disappointment without letting it get us down. Joy is so much bigger than happiness.

When people see this kind of joy in our lives it speaks volumes to them about the truth and power of the gospel message. People like Jimmy Houston show how joy can be a wonderful lure for believers and nonbelievers alike. If we serve God with a joyful spirit we will draw men and women to Him.

> The disciples were filled with joy and with the Holy Spirit.
> ACTS 13:52

SIX BULLS
AND A BOY

READ: 1 PETER 3

Gus Bess is a dynamic pastor and one who manifests a passion for everything he does, including bowhunting. When he was pastoring a church in the Bellingham, Washington, area he would often see elk while driving. One particular area seemed especially favorable to the elk. It was not uncommon to see them feeding in this small wooded area along the road. But when he stopped the car and stepped out, the elk would always escape through the forest into a clearing on the far side of the woods.

One day Gus decided to enlist the help of his 14-year-old son in setting a trap for the elk. But arriving at the usual spot, there were no elk to be seen. Gus thought for a moment, cooking up a strategy. "Danny," he said to his son, "give me about ten minutes to walk around to the back of the woods. Then, start walking toward the place where we have seen the elk feeding." He figured that if they were back in the woods this action might scare them out. When Gus saw them, he would be ready.

> For the Lord God is a sun and a shield: the Lord will give grace and glory: no good thing will he withhold from them that walk uprightly.
> PSALM 84:11 KJV

Gus moved quickly to his position and nocked an arrow. He waited for some time, wondering why it was taking his son so long to make his way through the woods. Suddenly he heard the familiar sound of hooves running across the forest floor. Listening intently, he realized that the sound was moving away from him. Concerned for Danny's safety, Gus ran through the woods to check on him. When he found him, Danny was standing perfectly still with his eyes bulging out of his head. "Son," Gus yelled, "are you all right?"

"Yeah, Dad," he answered, his voice unsteady. "I'm just scared."

"What happened?"

"Well, Dad, I did just what you said to do. I waited about ten minutes and started walking toward the woods. All of a sudden I came upon an entire herd of elk bedded down. Six big bull elk jumped to their feet and started acting like they wanted to fight me. They were snorting and digging at the ground. I became so frightened that all I could do was freeze – I couldn't move."

Gus figures that once the elk scented the boy they ran off. Danny was trying to do a good thing by helping his dad, but that helpfulness meant he had to endure some unexpected hardship: a face-to-face encounter with six angry bulls! From that point on, Gus and Danny always hunted together so that they could help and support one another if a dangerous situation arose. They learned the power of walking together. All of us need support and encouragement when we face trials and testing in our lives.

We need never fear the spiritual challenges that face us, for we have one who is always by our side. Jesus will be our guide and comforter in all the struggles of our life. He will see us through the darkest times. He will never leave us to face hardship all by ourselves, for He is always with us.

Fishing is the chance to wash
    one's soul with pure air,
        with the rush of a brook or
    with the shimmer of the sun on blue water.

Herbert Hoover

THE DIVINE SHOT

READ: GENESIS 11:1-9

Max Greiner, Jr. is a professional artist whose sculptures and paintings can be seen in galleries throughout the country. His beautiful, life-size bronze replicas of Christ washing Peter's feet and calling His fishermen-disciples are amazingly real and expressive. He is also an avid and much-respected bowhunter and one-time president of the National Bowhunter Education Foundation. In September 1997, Max joined six friends near McCall, Idaho, to bowhunt with guide Ray Rawls for the elusive black bear. The black bear is difficult to hunt because, while primarily a nocturnal animal, it can only be legally hunted during the day.

The group of hunters chose to hunt the bear by assigning each person a baited area and using dogs to find any roaming animals. After sitting patiently—and unproductively— in his tree stand over the bait for six days, Ray suggested that they try something new. His idea was that they would begin their hunt the next day by checking all the baited areas. That night, to fill some idle time, Max decided to pray. He didn't really consider himself the religious type and he wasn't really sure that God was listening, but his prayer was heartfelt: "Lord, I don't know if You are still working miracles and talking to Your children, but if You ever want to talk to me, I'd like to listen." Staring up into the dark night, this unbelieving hunter was suddenly impressed with this thought: *I'm going to kill a bear tomorrow morning. It will be the bear I have been hunting over my bait all week. It will be killed with a single arrow and will die instantly.*

> I do not trust in my bow, my sword does not bring me victory.
> PSALM 44:6

These thoughts shocked him. Where were they coming from? He had never had an experience like this.

The next morning he told everyone in camp about his unusual experience. After checking the other stations, Ray asked Max if he was ready to check his own station. Yes, he said. Moving to the area, the dogs picked up the scent of a bear. When they drew close they spotted it in a tree about 35 yards away.

Max let go with his arrows. The first two struck a limb nearby the bear. Max put another arrow in his 65-pound bow and pulled it back. Releasing it, the arrow flew to its mark, penetrating the heart and lungs of the bear, the broadhead lodging in the bear's spine and killing the 350-pound beast instantly.

The miracle of this story, Max says, is not that he got the bear, but what it taught him about God. The story reveals a God who hunts for the heart of a man and finds his mark. It tells of a God who is real and wants

to reveal Himself to His creatures. He will use any means necessary, even a bow, an arrow, and an answered prayer.

DRAWN BY THE LIGHT

READ: ACTS 9

As most fishermen know, trophy fish will tend to avoid the light during the day, hiding in the shadows or diving down to deeper depths. But things change in the evening. As night approaches, many species find light to be an invitation to finding an easy meal, because the baitfish, insects, and algae all tend to concentrate around a well-lit area.

> In the same way, let your light shine before men, that they may see your good deeds and praise your father in heaven.
> MATTHEW 5:16

My good friend Dick Gaumer, editor and outdoor writer, and I have often fished the Stockton, California delta late in the evenings. The late spring and summer evenings are always a good time to find a calm, well-lit bay teeming with fish. The big striped bass, black bass, American shad, and crappie in those waters will gather around the marina areas and quickly attack the surface plugs and mini jigs we present to them.

Fishermen in the time of Christ knew this truth and, consequently, did most of their fishing in the evening. They would build a fire in a highly polished brass pan which they placed in the middle of their boats. The reflected light would draw the fish to their boats, even from some distance away. And when the schools of fish came to the surface, nets were cast out and large catches could be made.

Therefore, when Jesus told His disciples (mostly fishermen) that He was the "light of men," his statement had an especially powerful impact. Still today, Jesus is the Light who will draw people to Him when we make others aware of the sacrifice He made for them on the cross. By the witness of our words and our lives we can show forth the light of Christ that will rescue men and women from their spiritual darkness. Go ahead, fishers of men…let your light shine!

TRIAL IN THE ALASKAN BUSH

READ: ROMANS 8:12-17

I 'll admit it. I've never liked tests.

Whether sitting in a classroom trying to remember the information given in a course of lectures, in a doctor's office as he administers a battery of examinations, or stranded on a remote mountain lake with bad weather and inadequate supplies, it is usually not pleasant to be tested. But sometimes a test will do us a great deal of good. The very fact that we emerge victoriously from a test or trial can help inspire great confidence in the One who has brought us through it all. It can build and strengthen our faith.

My hunting partner, John, and I had saved all year so that we could afford our 1996 Alaskan caribou and bear hunt. We were filled with anticipation for months before. When our plane set us down near a remote mountain lake we thought at first that we had arrived in paradise. But then things started to go wrong. First, John began to have difficulty breathing. Apparently all the mold and fungus surrounding our area had reactivated some old allergy problems. He quickly became very weak and all attempts to medicate him failed to do any real good. He was in no shape to hunt.

> Consider it pure joy, my brothers, whenever you face trials of many kinds, because you know that the testing of your faith develops perseverance. Perseverance must finish its work so that you may be mature and complete, not lacking anything.
>
> JAMES 1:2,3

Then the weather took a drastic turn for the worse. A heavy storm shook our little tent so hard that we thought it would collapse and caused branches of nearby trees to fall on our expensive equipment. The rain soaked us and our matches and scared away any animals that might have been in the area. The animals had done what we decided we must do—leave the area behind. We placed a distress signal on the ground and hailed a small plane. A few hours later we were picked up,

soaked to the bone and very disappointed. All the money and anticipation seemed to go for nothing.

Some might have decided to give up this kind of hunting all together. After all, if there is no guarantee of comfort and success, why not spend your resources in a more profitable manner? Why not stay home where the conditions were more predictable? But that was not our attitude. We knew that life is made up of disappointments as well as successes. Things don't always go the way we envision them, but that should never cause us to give up. We should emerge from times of testing with a commitment to keep on going. In fact, I'm already looking forward to my next opportunity to hunt in Alaska. Maybe next time things will go a little closer to the plan!

Because we know that everything—both the bad and the good we experience—is under the providence of God, we must trust that He uses the tests and trials of our lives to make us into the kind of people He wants us to be. The difficult times are part of His ultimate plan for our lives. As Charles

Spurgeon once wrote, "Trials lurk on every road. Everywhere, above and beneath, we are beset and surrounded with danger. Yet no shower falls unprompted from the threatening cloud. Every raindrop has its orders before it falls. The trials that come from God are sent to prove and strengthen our graces. They illustrate the power of divine grace to test the genuineness of our virtues and add to their energy."

What trials and tests are you experiencing in your life? Friend, remember that all your blessings and trials are alike from the hand of your heavenly Father. Don't give up or despair, but instead listen for what God may have to teach you through your difficulties. Ultimately, that is how we pass the test!

THE MASTER GUIDE

READ: PSALM 25:5

There are few things that will make fishing more enjoyable than to do it with an experienced fishing guide. The two most important qualities a guide brings to his clients are a working knowledge of local "hot spots," and an encouraging spirit. His ability to quickly locate where the fish are and to select the right tackle will save folks a lot of time and frustration. Once he's located the fish, it is important for the guide to encourage the anglers so that they fish with confidence. You can have the right location and the right tackle, but you also need the inspiration of an encouraging guide.

Whenever I'm guiding others, I make it a priority to see that my clients are being inspired about what they are doing. I have learned that if they believe, it is much more likely that they will receive. For example, an expectant cast will have a much greater chance of landing a fish than one that is simply dunked in the water. If we really believe that we are going to catch a fish, we stand ready to work the lure in a tempting manner and strike at the most appropriate time.

As fishers of men we look to Jesus Christ as the ultimate Master Guide. His disciples knew that there was no one who knew the souls of men like He did. He often used analogies from fishing to impart to them the truths of His eternal kingdom. He showed them that they must leave their musty nets to pursue a life of netting souls. He constantly encouraged his disciples to trust in His power to bring men to salvation.

There will be no greater reward than to stand with the Master Guide on the grandstands of heaven to welcome those souls who were caught by our testimonies and landed by His Spirit. Peter Marshall, former chaplain of the U.S. Senate, once said, "Fishing for fish is pulling fish out of life into death. Fishing for men is pulling men from death unto life." Think about it for a moment: What are you fishing for in your life? Who are you depending upon as your guide?

> The Lord will guide you always.
>
> ISAIAH 58:11

BEAR COUNTRY

READ: PSALM 108:6

On one of my many trips to Alaska, I took a group of dads and their sons to a remote lake about an hour's plane ride from our base camp in the Kenai area. As the floatplane gently touched down on the pristine lake you could feel the rising anticipation. We split up to find good fishing holes, so the guide and I decided that as a special treat we would take the two youngest boys to a small island located just off a major salmon run. The current there was swift and the water deep around this little strip of land.

Over the next couple of hours we landed some trophy sockeye salmon, keeping the two larger ones to mount. But we soon learned that we were not the only ones fishing in this area. Just down river from our location we spotted a large grizzly bear, who was feeding on the same salmon we were trying to catch. As he moved closer to us, it was obvious he had spotted our beached salmon. He must have thought these beautiful fish would make a fine snack. And we were in his way.

It did not take long for him to get too close for comfort. Seeing the 450-pound bear, I yelled to the guide to bring his rubber raft down to where we were. We needed to get out of there fast! The guide rowed the boat down and we jumped in. In his hurry, though, the guide pulled a little too hard on the starter cord for the engine and it snapped off in his hands. We had to do some fast and vigorous paddling to put a safe distance between ourselves and the grizzly. As a precaution, I pulled out my .44 magnum so I would be prepared in case the bear decided to charge. Thankfully, I didn't have to use it. In a short time we were safely out of the bear's territory.

> Resist [Satan], standing firm in the faith, because you know that your brothers throughout the world are undergoing the same kind of sufferings.
> 1 PETER 5:9

Bear attacks are one of the hazards of being in the wilderness. Anytime you are in bear country you need to know what to do to outsmart these ferocious animals. Wade Knowland, a hunting guide whom I greatly respect, suggests the following things you can do to protect yourself against a bear attack. Keep these in mind next time you are in bear country:

1. Always stay in a small group. When two or more people are together the likelihood of bear attacks drops significantly.

2. Make plenty of noise when traveling through the woods. Bears will generally leave an area where human beings are present.

3. Seal all your food supplies and garbage in plastic bags, and keep edible items out of your sleeping quarters. Most bears attack because they are interested in your food, not you.

4. When you encounter a bear, move slowly upwind from his location. Give them plenty of space and never get between a mother bear and her cubs.

5. Carry a large-caliber firearm and/or some bear spray-repellent. Use these only as a last resort.

Just as bears present a potential danger to the outdoorsman, and are therefore worthy of our utmost caution and respect, so the Christian must not overlook the enemy we face in our spiritual life. If we don't pay attention to the danger he poses, we are likely to fall prey to his wiles and temptations. Peter reminded the believers of the early church about the predatory quality of Satan: "Be self-controlled and alert. Your enemy the devil prowls around like a roaring lion looking for someone to devour" (1 Peter 5:8).

Just as the best defense against bear attacks is an awareness of the danger they present, so the best defense against the attacks of the evil one is to be aware and prepared. Our spiritual survival in times of temptation depends upon three things: first, knowing when to flee, (recognizing those situations where we are sure to be defeated if we do not remove ourselves from the temptation); second, knowing the Word of God and how to use it to defeat our spiritual foe; and third, the help and assistance of our brothers and sisters in the Lord who will hold us up in prayer and fellowship. When traveling in bear country or devil country we need to be alert, be prepared, and be ready to flee.

God never did make
a more calm, quiet, innocent
recreation than angling.

IZAAK WALTON

GETTING SKUNKED AT FLY-FISHING

READ: 1 TIMOTHY 1:18

I 'll never forget the story Russell Thornberry told about the time he got skunked at fly fishing. Russell was guiding two fly fishermen on the famous Bow River, and it was just "one of those ugly days." The wind was incredibly strong and the weather kept changing—mostly for the worst! "Things were not going well at all," Russell says. "You couldn't even buy a fish—it was that bad!" By the time they all stopped for lunch, no one had managed even a tentative nibble.

> Fight the good fight of the faith. Take hold of
> the eternal life to which you were called
> when you made your good confession
> in the presence of many witnesses.
>
> 1 TIMOTHY 6:12

Normally, Russell didn't fish himself while he was guiding clients. His job, he felt, was to help them have the best possible experience, so he concentrated on figuring out where the fish were and helping his clients improve their technique.

But because the conditions were so tough on this particular outing, he decided to depart from his usual way of doing things. He figured that if he could use one of his secret fly patterns, then maybe, just maybe, he could charm a fish into hitting his fly. And if that was successful, then he could prove to his disheartened clients that fish really did exist in the Bow River.

Russell waded down to a section of the river where the grass banks formed a high wall on one side of the waterway. But as he tried to cast out his line, the wind caught it and whipped it back onto the grassy bank. He tried it again. And again. Each of six times the grass caught his line and stole his fly. But still he persevered. He would not give up.

On the seventh cast, he snagged again and had to give a mighty tug to free his line. When he jerked his rod forward, he felt something funny. There was a great deal of weight on the line. Turning to check it out, he gave another strong tug, only to see a ball of black-and-white fur flying off the bank and right over his head. He ducked just in time, as a poor old skunk landed in the river!

Apparently the skunk had mistaken the imitation grasshopper for the real thing and had sampled a bit of Russell's streamer fly. Both Russell and the skunk were unspeakably disappointed!

All of us have had those days where we feel "skunked," where nothing seems to go right; days when we wish we had just stayed in bed. But when we feel this way, we need to remember that our God is a mighty God and that He encourages us to keep on keepin' on. When we feel that life is just too much of a battle, we need to remember the words of the apostle Paul as he wrote to the Corinthian Christians, reminding them of the need for diligence and perseverance in the midst of their morally lax society. "I do not fight like a man beating the air," he wrote. "No, I beat my body and

make it my slave so that after I have preached to others, I myself will not be disqualified for the prize" (1 Corinthians 9:26,27). Paul knew that it could be a temptation to give up and give in on those days when we feel skunked. But he encouraged us to battle on!

What battle are you fighting? You can have victory over the temptations in your life if you remain faithful to God's Word and persist in the good fight of faith. Don't give up…even when you feel skunked!

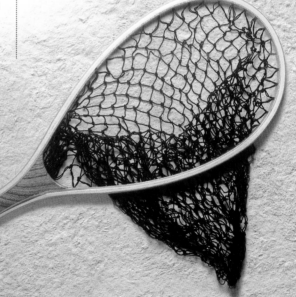

PARABLE OF THE BUFFALO

READ: MATTHEW 23

Sometimes in life we get a "bad rap." None of us is faultless or totally free from blame, but it is very frustrating when we get accused for something that is not our fault. Hunters should be very familiar with the reality of getting a "bad rap." There are people who are so opposed to this sportsman's hobby that they are very quick to make unfounded accusations. It has been said, for example, that hunters are to blame for the dwindling populations of endangered species in our world. If this was true, it would be a very serious problem. But actually, sportsmen not only are not to blame for the diminishing populations of endangered species, they have actually been at the forefront of working to preserve fish and wildlife.

> Blessed are those who are persecuted because of righteousness, for theirs is the kingdom of heaven.
> MATTHEW 5:10

The kind of regulated sports hunting that is practiced today has never brought a single species close to extinction. One need only to consider the fate of the American buffalo (bison) to understand the realities behind hunting's "bad rap." When the first Europeans arrived in North America, the buffaloes numbered between 60 and 80 million. By the time sportsmen were able to persuade the U.S. Congress to enact laws for the protection of the species, their numbers had been reduced to about 600 animals.

Why did the numbers fall so precipitously? What happened to the buffaloes? It was certainly not the fault of the sportsman enjoying his hobby. The culprits were the market hunters, whose greed and recklessness reduced the great herds of the 1800s to a small population. The buffalo were not killed for sport. In fact, it is the efforts spearheaded by sportsmen that made Congress finally take the issue seriously. Now, thanks to the foresight of these sportsmen, more than 130,000 head roam freely in parks and bison ranges. Their population is rebuilding.

Without the assistance of sportsmen's organizations, the wild turkey, elk, and duck populations would be threatened as well. We can thank these associations for all they have done to foster ethical hunting and wildlife conservation. They have helped us to fulfill God's command as it is recorded in Genesis 1:28: "God blessed them and said to them, 'Be fruitful and increase in number; fill the earth and subdue it. Rule over the fish of the sea and the birds of the air and over every living creature that moves on the ground.'" Responsible stewardship has been the key to wildlife conservation.

As believers we also know the power of a "bad rap." We are often accused of hypocrisy (or worse!) by those who are the enemies of the gospel. We should not be surprised at this response, for even Christ was accused of hypocrisy by the religious leaders of His time. We are accused of being judgmental when we are only trying to stand firmly for God's commandments, of being "holier than thou" when we strive only to do the right thing.

The next time someone gives you a "bad rap" because of your commitment to the gospel, consider their words carefully. They may have noticed something about you that you have not seen about yourself! We can sometimes be blind to our own shortcomings. But if the criticism is unjust, consider its source. As believers we will not be immune to criticism, attack, or persecution. We must stand firmly in our convictions and rest in the knowledge that God's approval far outweighs the "bad raps" which might be directed toward us.

"TOUGH BITE" DAYS

READ: JAMES 5:11

I am often asked who has contributed most to the passion I have for the sport of fishing. I don't have to think long to answer this question. Despite all the wonderful knowledge and enthusiasm of many sponsors, mentors, and professionals, I would have to say that Elmer Etter, my father-in-law, has influenced my love of fishing more than anyone else. Elmer was a surface-plug fisherman from Indiana, and although he has been dead for almost twenty years, there is not a fishing trip that goes by that I don't apply some of his wise counsel.

> To those who by persistence in doing good seek glory, honor, and immortality, he will give eternal life.
> ROMANS 2:7

On "tough bite" days, when the fish seem resistant to the usual bait, most folks would switch to natural baits such as worms, crawfish, or frogs to tempt the stubborn bass. Not Elmer. When fishing with him on such days we would throw those Creek Club Injured Minnows and Hula Popper Frog surface lures until our arms felt ready to fall off. We would try many different types of rhythms, actions, colors, sizes, speeds, and directions in quest of the right combination that would stimulate a bite. Elmer didn't give up easily. His motto was, "Just keep on chuckin' and windin'—there's a fish out there somewhere who will bite."

When it comes to character development, this is also good advice. It doesn't come easily and sometimes it doesn't seem like any change at all is happening. These are the times when we need to keep on chuckin' and windin'. We need to be persistent, staying steady and continuous in our course, pursuing that which is good with a passion even when change seems slow. We must run the course of life steadily and patiently. As the writer of Hebrews encourages us, "Since we are surrounded by such a great cloud of witnesses, let us throw off everything that hinders and the sin that so easily entangles, and let us run with perseverance the race marked out for us" (Hebrews 12:1).

If you are having a "tough bite" day, remember the advice from Hebrews and ol' Elmer—just keep chuckin' and windin'.

Snag Proof Popper

THE HOLINESS OF THE HUNT

READ: GENESIS 1

The actions of some irresponsible hunters have given the sport a bad name in the minds of many nonhunters. Over the years I have watched as a gap in understanding has grown. Some people actually consider hunting a barbaric ritual that has no place in modern, civilized society. They think that game is being wastefully slaughtered for selfish gain. What they do not comprehend is the strong sense of stewardship over God's creation that so many hunters feel.

As a prolific hunter, I have a deep love for all God has created. I also know from the book of Genesis that God gave man dominion over all His creation, with the purpose that he might enjoy the creation and use its creatures to sustain his life. Throughout the Scriptures, animals have provided a means for sacrifice, clothing, and food. We are charged with the responsibility for being good stewards over what God has given to us.

> Everything that lives and moves will be food for you.
>
> GENESIS 9:3

Sometimes that stewardship involves responsible management of all the gifts we are given. Numerous countries have severe problems maintaining their vegetation and agricultural resources because they fail to see the God-given responsibility to keep nature in balance. Without controlled hunting we would face oversized populations of certain animals which would cause exhaustion of resources, overcrowding, endangerment of humans or livestock, and disease.

Dr. Tom C. Rakow and John D. Morgan are two well-respected pastors as well as avid outdoorsmen. Each of them has written essays to help us better understand God's Word in relation to hunting. From them I have learned that hunting is among the most ancient of outdoor skills. God first granted permission to hunt 4000 years ago. Sometime after the flood in Noah's day (Genesis 6-9) and before the confusion of languages at Babel (Genesis 11:1-9), a man named Nimrod appeared on the stage of human history. The Bible says concerning him, "He was a mighty hunter before the Lord" (Genesis 10:9).

We find other examples later in the biblical record. Esau was a "skillful hunter" (Genesis 25:27). David, while still a young shepherd, killed wild animals to protect his flock. But the most compelling evidence that hunting was ordained by God comes in His words to Noah after the ark landed: "Everything that lives and moves will be food for you. Just as I gave you the green plants, I now give you everything" (Genesis 9:3). He later instructed the Hebrews how to properly prepare kills for human consumption (Leviticus 17:13), and granted permission for Jews to eat various wild game (Deuteronomy 14:5). Hunting, therefore, is something that has been part of human life since the very beginning, and God gave it to us so that we could benefit from it and enjoy it. But it comes with the responsibility of stewardship.

Because of this responsibility, I am vitally concerned about what is happening to wildlife all around the world. Hunters should oppose senseless and irresponsible slaughter and support rational proposals for the protection of wildlife populations. We should be at the forefront of protecting that for which God has given us responsibility. With privilege always comes responsibility.

WHY HUNTING IS HEALTHY FOR HUMANS

READ: PSALM 96

Some people think that hunting is fun, and it is. But it is more than that. Hunting provides an opportunity to bond with nature in a special, life-giving way. As you rise early in the morning and make your way in the dark to your tree stand, anticipation fills the air. The owls are making their final pass over the fields, hooting and howling as they discuss your arrival. The chill of the morning mist settles on the back of your neck as rays of light begin to appear on the eastern horizon.

Your eyes strain to spot any movement as the dull brown and gray tones of the fall become the background for your drama. After a couple hours surveying the woods, moving your eyes back and forth, you become aware of everything around you. Any new shape, sound, or movement comes to your attention.

Then, seemingly out of nowhere, a deer appears. Deer have a knack for these sudden appearances, as they move so stealthily. When you first spot the deer, your heart begins to race, your eyes begin to bulge, and your palms begin to sweat. You feel every heartbeat in your throat. You are so very alive.

That is part of the joy of hunting, but its worth doesn't end there. Steve Chapman has done a masterful job of describing the experience of deer hunting in his book, *A Look at Life from a Deer Stand*. In the book, Steve points to three things we can gain from par-

1 *A harvest of healthy meat*. Deer meat is very lean and free from the toxic chemicals that often are present in store-bought goods. Venison is such a wonderful food source. Plus, it's easy to justify hunting for venison when beef sells for three dollars a pound.

2 *A harvest of mental medicine*. The opportunity to relish the peace of nature and to escape the business of our hectic everyday lives is another of the joys of hunting. We have the pleasure of relaxing in the outdoors, which improves our psychological well-being in a way that the psychiatrist's couch never could.

3 *A harvest of truths*. Steve relates, "While it's a fact that each time I go out I learn something new about a hunting tactic or a technical improvement to my equipment, there are greater lessons about life that I 'bagged' that are now mounted on the wall of my heart." The long hours of "think time" hunting provides give us a chance to work through life's priorities and realize what is really important. God most often speaks to me when I'm best able to listen.

> As the deer pants for streams of water, so my soul pants for you, O God.
> PSALM 42:1

Use your hunting experience as a time to commune with the living God. The spiritual trophies you will

10 GREAT TRUTHS FOR FISHING & LIFE

"After all these years I still feel like a boy
when I'm on a stream or lake."

JIMMY CARTER

"Men learn best when they teach others."

SENECA

"Angling may be said to be like mathematics
in that it can never fully be learnt."

IZAAK WALTON

"If people concentrated on the
really important things in life,
there'd be a shortage of fishing poles."

DOUG LARSON

"Nature is the art of God."

DANTE

"Successful hunters and fishermen
are precise observers of the world around them.
They have to be in order to be successful."

GEORGE REIGER

"Ten percent of all fishermen
catch ninety percent of all the fish.
They find these fish in an area
which makes up only ten percent
of the lake, river, or pond."

JIM GRASSI

"It's what you learn after
you know it all that counts."

HARRY TRUMAN

"The greatest fishing secret ever. Patience!"

DONALD JACK ANDERSON

"There is certainly something in fishing
that tends to produce a gentleness
of spirit and a pure sincerity of mind."

WASHINGTON IRVING

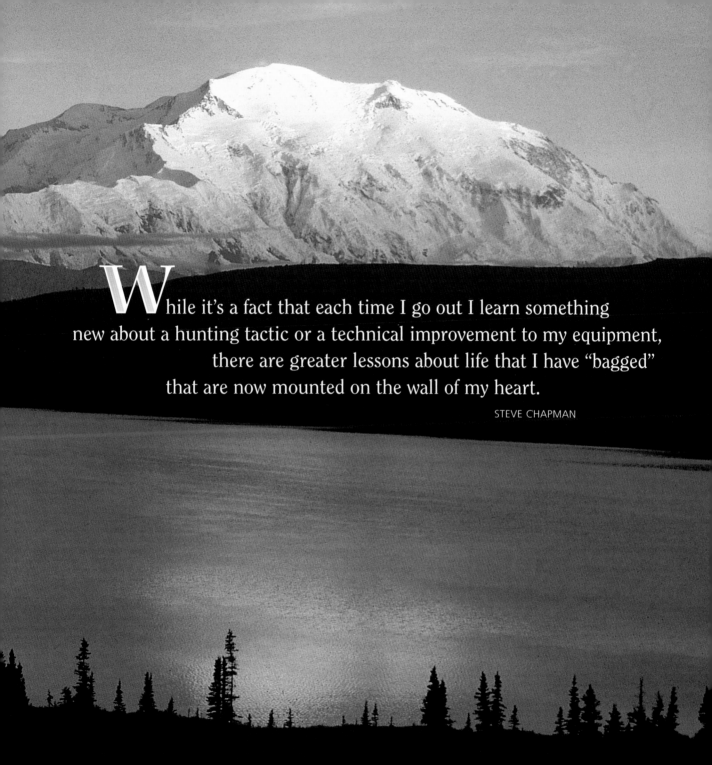

While it's a fact that each time I go out I learn something new about a hunting tactic or a technical improvement to my equipment, there are greater lessons about life that I have "bagged" that are now mounted on the wall of my heart.

STEVE CHAPMAN

FLYING IN THE FOG

READ: PSALM 48:14

Whenever I visit Alaska, I bring along extra antacids.

I've always enjoyed flying, but the experience of being in a small plane, weaving in and out around jagged mountain peaks in the clouds and dense fog, is just a little more excitement than I really need. (Though I must admit that it does wonders for improving my prayer life!)

On one recent trip to Alaska, a small commercial plane was scheduled to take us from our hunting adventure near Lake Clark to the airport in Anchorage. After boarding, the pilot received instructions on how to navigate through the tricky Inland Passage. This narrow passage requires full concentration on the part of the pilot due to the numerous changes in elevation and direction.

Shortly after takeoff, the pilot directed our craft toward the misty canyons of the passage. Within minutes it became apparent that the limited visibility was going to create a real problem. As we flew straight into fog, I felt the beads of sweat break out on my forehead. I couldn't help but wonder if the pilot was really prepared for the task of getting us through safely.

What I didn't consider was that the pilot would not have to do it alone. Realizing the potential hazards, he decided to climb to an altitude where he would be able to pick up the air-traffic controller's radio signal. Once he was able to receive these directions, the pilot flew smoothly and confidently to our destination. (I wasn't quite as confident, so I got a lot of praying done!)

That adventure reminded me of the way that God uses the Holy Spirit to help guide His children. But we must always remember that it is God's mission we are undertaking, not our own. I once heard a wise pastor say, "God didn't give us the Holy Spirit so that the Holy Spirit could help us achieve our purposes. God gave us the Holy Spirit so that the Holy Spirit could help us achieve God's purposes." How often do we pray for the Lord to help us accomplish our goals, bless our directions, and honor our chosen path, when our real call is to follow His directions. Just like the air-traffic controller, God will show us the best path to follow to achieve what He has in mind for us.

Proverbs 3:5,6 contains a wonderful admonition: "Trust in the LORD with all your heart, and lean not on your own understanding; in all your ways acknowledge him, and he will make your paths straight." Navigating through our lives is a lot like flying through a cloudy mountain range. We must rely on someone else to keep us on track. The pilot must depend on the air-traffic controller. Sometimes the controller dictates a course that the pilot would not have chosen—he may have to circle or fly in another direction for awhile. But the pilot doesn't question the controller's judgment and contemplate going his own way. That could be disastrous! His lack of trust could lead him into denser fog, low-lying electrical lines, or oncoming commercial traffic that would end his trip in a hurry. The pilot trusts the controller because the controller sees the bigger picture, knows what lies ahead, and can safely determine the best way to reach the destination.

Likewise, we must trust our Divine Controller, the One who sees what we cannot see. He is our omnipotent (all-knowing) guide through all the fog and confusion of our life. The future is history, not mystery, for God.

> Do not cast me from your presence or take your Holy Spirit from me.
> PSALM 51:11

CHECKING YOUR GEAR

READ: 1 CORINTHIANS 12

Every occupation has its tools of the trade: a carpenter uses hammer and nails; a mason depends upon trowels and mixing boards; an accountant stores plenty of paper, pens, and adding machine tape so he can complete his task. An archer is no different. His bow, arrows, and quiver are the tools he needs to pursue his passion in the outdoors.

> Do not neglect your gift.
>
> 1 TIMOTHY 4:14

Developing archery skills is a lot like the practice of disciple-making. Both require specialized "tools of the trade."

1. ATTITUDE. Archers must maintain a mature and positive outlook as they seek to master their sport. Archery is not easy. Confidence develops only as the archer becomes more experienced. It takes time and effort. To become a mature and productive Christian we must expend time and effort.

2. EQUIPMENT. To master any sport you must have the right equipment and keep it properly maintained. The archer's bow must be tuned, his arrow straight, and his release functioning properly in order to make that perfect shot. In similar fashion, a Christian's life and theology must be balanced and shaped with prayer, teaching, fellowship, meditation, rest, devotion, and love (1 Peter 1:13). These are the tools of Christian growth.

3. BOW. Whether an archer uses a recurve or compound bow, he considers it an extension of himself. The bow is effective only if and when the archer picks it up and uses it for its intended purpose. Without an archer and an arrow, the bow is useless. Each believer is promised at least one spiritual gift which defines his service to the church: pastoring, teaching, serving, speaking prophecy, giving, etc. These gifts blend naturally with our attitudes, temperaments, innate talents, and learned skills to ignite spiritual passion in our hearts. But the power of the gift, as with the archer's bow, is dormant until put to use (1 Corinthians 12).

4. ARROWS. An arrow has five main components. Each is critical for accurate flight. The arrow

shaft must be straight and free of blemish as our walk before God must be pure (Matthew 7:13,14). The broadhead must be sharp enough to penetrate a target as the Word of God can pierce the soul and spirit (Hebrews 4:12). The nock-attachment point, like our convictions, must hold fast (Hebrews 10:23). Our strength must be as stable and supple as an arrow's spine (1 Chronicles 16:11). The fletchings guide the arrow's flight just as the Holy Spirit, when invited, guides our lives (John 16:13).

5. QUIVER. A quiver allows the archer to store his arrows in an organized and safe manner until he needs them. In a similiar fashion the arrows of life are our testimonies and are stored in our hearts and minds. They can be released

in a timely manner in order to hit the target of a spiritual void in another person's life.

Have you checked your "spiritual gear" lately to see if it is in proper working order? God has provided us with the equipment we need for spiritual living, but we must take up these tools and use them. Like the archer, let us use these gifts to take aim at the target of spiritual maturity.

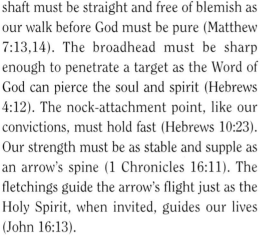

My advice then to the young is: Learn the art of hunting if you desire to grow up to be good men, good in everything which is perfect in thought, word and deed. The first efforts of a youth emerging from boyhood should be directed to the chase. If you can succeed in that, all else will seem easy to you.

XENOPHON

FROM CANE POLE TO CASTING ROD

READ: JUDE 24,25

One of the wonderful truths about fishing is that you will never learn everything there is to know about this dynamic sport. There are so many types of fishing, species of fish, and places to fish that you can literally spend a lifetime investing yourself in the sport and still not become an expert. The more you learn, the more you realize what you have yet to learn!

Most of us who have become passionate about fishing started off the same way. The ol' cane pole or spin-cast combo allowed us to fish for pan-size fish like blue-gill, crappie, perch, or sunfish on some isolated cove or pond. After a while we want more challenge, so we progress to open-face spinning combinations and begin to seek out bass and trout, using plugs, soft plastics, jigs, spoons, and spinners. Next, we might move on to mastering the bait-casting reel. And while we may throw the same type of lures, we begin to develop more control and flex-ibility in our casting techniques. Spunky steelhead, salmon, striped bass, and other hard-fighting species are the targets of our newfound skills.

> He who establishes us
> with you in Christ
> and anointed us is God.
> 2 CORINTHIANS 1:21 NASB

Finally, we are ready to take on the most challeng-ing dimension of the sport: fly-fishing. The depth of knowledge about various kinds of flies and pre-sentations that fly-fishing requires forces us to learn new skills. The study, skill, and concentration that it requires can exhaust any fisherman, no mat-ter how avid. But there are many rewards for the fisherman who perseveres in learning this particular form of fishing.

Is not the Christian life a lot like this? We progress by stages, deeper and deeper, into the depths of a walk with Christ. First, we meet Christ. That first meet-ing is life-changing, as it was for those first-century fisher-men, Peter, James, and John. After Jesus instructed them to put their nets into deep water, they enjoyed an astonishing catch—and they recognized who was speaking to them. "Don't be afraid," He said. "From now on you will catch men" (Luke 5:10). Each of us has heard a similar call, and like those early disciples we "left everything and followed him."

Although the disciples lived and traveled with Jesus, saw Him do many miracles, and heard the powerful words He spoke, they still needed to be challenged with making Him first in their hearts and growing into a more committed life with the Savior. When Jesus asked them, "Who do you say that I am?" He was challenging them to commit to a deeper level of understanding and a deeper level of sacrifice. What about you? How would you answer if Jesus posed this question to you? Is He just the focus of a set of religious beliefs or have you made Him the center of your life?

We must never come to the place in our Christian lives where we think we have *arrived*. We must never think that we know it all. There is always more to learn, more to experience, more to let God do in His work of changing us into the likeness of His Son. Let us never become complacent about our relationship with God or satisfied with what we know. Let us launch out into the depths!

FISHING FOR HUMILITY

READ: PROVERBS 8:13

Sometimes great success can bring with it the danger of great pride. Just ask Daryl Christensen. A walleye fisherman for many years, Daryl has chalked up numerous victories in professional fishing tournaments. Few could boast of the kind of knowledge Daryl had of that particular species of fish. But he tells a sobering story about how he learned the dangers of pride.

One overcast June day several years ago, Daryl and his amateur fishing partner were fishing a pro-am tournament on Mille Lacs Lake. They were about six miles offshore when they found a "honey hole," a place where the walleye seemed to be stacked up like cordwood. Daryl smiled to think that the tournament victory would certainly be theirs.

Hearing a rumble in the distance, he looked up, spotting a thunderhead making its way across the lake in their direction. Soon it would be right over their position. Daryl's partner suggested that it was time to head for safety, but Daryl was worried that they might not be able to find this particular hot spot again. He told his partner not to worry. As the dark clouds rumbled nearer, Daryl joked, "I'm ready if God wants to take me."

"Well, I'm not," answered his partner.

> As God's chosen people, holy and dearly loved, clothe yourselves with compassion, kindness, humility, gentleness and patience.
> COLOSSIANS 3:12

Daryl saw that the amateur needed some convincing. "I have stayed out in similar situations before with no problem," he arrogantly asserted, sure he knew best. Then, just as he was about to cast, a bolt of lightning split the sky hitting his seven-foot graphite pole. The charge knocked Daryl off his feet and rendered him unconscious for several minutes. A painful lesson, indeed!

Our pride has a way of endangering our common sense and our spiritual well-being. Tucked away in the latter part of the Old Testament is a little four-chapter-long book about a prophet named Jonah. He, too, had a problem with pride which stemmed from his accomplishments as a "successful prophet." We all know what happened to him as a result of deciding that he knew better than God what he should be doing with his life. When he went the opposite direction from what God had commanded, he ended up getting a special booking from God with an alternative method of travel—the belly of a giant fish!

We should strive to be obedient to what God (and sometimes our common sense) tells us, not arrogantly thinking that we are above falling into great dangers, both physical and spiritual. Pride will produce sin in our lives because it tells us that we know our path better than God does. If we act in humility, we can avoid the kind of fish story that was experienced by Daryl and Jonah!

JIM'S DEADLY DOZEN (+1) NORTH AMERICAN LURES

Creek Chub-Perch Injured Minnow

Fred Arbogast-Frog Hula Popper

Panther Martin-Black and Gold Spinner

Strike King-White and Chartreuse Willow Leaf Spinner Bait

Lew Eppinger's-Red and White Dardevle Spoon

Strom Lures Wiggle Wart-Blueback

Blue Fox Pixie Lure-Gold/Red

Rebel Deep Diving Chrome and Black Minnow

Gene Larew-Black and Chartreuse Ring Worm 6"

Snag Proof Tournament Frog

Cordell Spot-Chrome and Black

Gene Larew-Melon and Orange 6" Craw

Blakemore Road Runner-Black and Chartreuse

THE MIRACLES DOWN UNDER

READ: ISAIAH 61:10,11

God loves to confound unbelievers, to give them little glimpses of the truth that shake up their patterns of unbelief. I can imagine the surprise those seasoned first-century fishermen felt when they hauled two boatloads of fish out of the waters of the Sea of Galilee. Simon Peter and his fishing partners had been fishing unsuccessfully the whole day until, at a word from Jesus, they suddenly found their nets full to bursting. This demonstration of God's power over His creation made believers out of them!

Sometimes God seems to take great delight in showing what He can do in answer to our prayers. I remember my first trip to New Zealand, where I had gone as part of a Kiwi marketing strategy to entice American fishermen into vacations there. The plan was to film me in action using my ultralight fishing techniques on a variety of species and develop programs and promotional tapes that we could use to attract new fly and spin fishermen to the pristine waters of this beautiful country.

The organizers started me off fishing for world-class striped marlin, but the problem was that the marlin just weren't biting. The cameras were rolling, but there wasn't much to record! The camera crew became increasingly dubious that we could actually catch and release a trophy marlin within the one-day window we had set for ourselves. Then, just five minutes before the first day's fishing was to end, my Christian fishing partners and I prayed that God would demonstrate His power over the situation. He did. Within minutes a trophy striped marlin hit our ultralight rod. It took a 45-minute fight to land and then release this monster 265-pound fish on camera. What great footage we got!

WHITE POINTER

> For the Lord takes
> delight in his people;
> he crowns the humble
> with salvation.
>
> PSALM 149:4

The next day God provided some of the hottest action ever recorded of offshore fishing, and two days after that some fabulous film of me catching several trophy trout on ultralight tackle. (And these trout were caught in a stream that has a solid reputation for being contrary to spin fishermen!) Later that same afternoon, I decided to try my hand at fly-fishing. Because the bank was very brushy and there was a bend in the river, it seemed that the task of attracting those brown trout that feed on the surface would be nearly impossible. But through a series of miraculous events and a puff of breeze at a critical moment, I landed and released on camera a wild and woolly six-pound trout that has now appeared on several featured videos. Prayer had turned around our previously unsuccessful expedition.

God takes great delight in pleasing His children and demonstrating His authority over the universe He made. The testimony resulting from my experiences "down under" was more a demonstration of God's presence and power than of my skill as an angler. My years of experience and depth of skill as a fisherman simply could not account for what I experienced in those few days of phenomenal fishing. Sometimes things happen in our lives that we can only credit to the power of God. And they become a testimony to even the hardest heart that God is alive!

I have never been happier, more exhilarated, at peace, rested, inspired, and aware of the grandeur of the universe and the greatness of God than when I find myself in a natural setting not much changed from the way He made it.

JIMMY CARTER

THE ENEMY IN OUR SIGHTS: DESPAIR

READ: ISAIAH 40:31

Bill Roades was on a roll. It was 1985 and he had established himself on the cutting edge of medical science as a heart and lung technician and operator. He was in good health, happily married, and financially secure. In addition, Bill was an avid hunter who had established a local record among bow hunters by shooting at least one buck a year for four years in a row. Few could match his archery skills.

But one day his world came crashing down. It was a warm summer afternoon when his brother invited him to take his motorcycle for a ride. He jumped on the cycle and decided to see what it could do. He smiled as the wind whipped his face, the pavement rushing by underneath the wheels of the powerful machine. But rounding a blind corner as he approached a bridge, he knew he was in trouble. He misjudged the bend and smashed his right shoulder against a large steel girder. In a split second the nerves from his arm were torn away from his spinal column. The result was instantaneous paralysis.

A series of three surgeries saved his life, but Bill faced a long recuperation and the permanent loss of the use of his arm. The very thought of losing his arm filled him with thoughts of despair, denial, and deep grief. "You mourn the loss of your arm the way you would mourn the death of a friend," he said. With the loss of his arm, he wondered if a lot of the things he most enjoyed in life would also be lost. Feelings of despair stared him in the face.

As the months passed, Bill renewed his interest in spiritual things and found his depression giving way to a new perspective. He realized that God

disabled person who told him how to modify a compound bow to accommodate a nylon mouthpiece on the string. Now, using his teeth and a modified anchor point, Bill is able to shoot a 60-pound compound bow and has been successful in taking some nice deer with it.

Each time he pulls back the bowstring and feels the force of the draw, he is reminded that God's strength is the real power behind his life. Bill has found that he can appropriate God's energy where his own is inadequate. It starts with realizing that despair is our enemy and then making the decision to defeat it with God's power and perspective.

wasn't through with him yet. Despite the fact that he had lost his occupation, his robust physical appearance, and his ability to do many things, he determined to move ahead with his life. Bill began to defeat despair when he got it in his sights and took dead center aim at it. He claimed God's promise, "I can do all things through Him who strengthens me" (Philippians 4:13).

With that assurance he began to think about his favorite pastime: archery. He contacted another

DANGEROUS DECOYS

READ: ACTS 17:11

The area around my home is a perfect place to observe wildlife. I am blessed to be living in an environment which is surrounded by open space, broken only by intermittent stands of trees. It is the ideal arena in which to study animal life and test different methods for attracting them. From the ground and from tree stands, I have viewed and filmed many creatures in order to better understand their habits, behavior, and characteristics. Some of my sponsors have even provided products for me to test in my outdoor laboratory. I've experimented with assorted game calls, chemical scents, and life-size decoys to lure these critters into my area. Through all of this, one of my most surprising discoveries has been the amazing gullibility of some animals.

> There will be false teachers among you. They will secretly introduce destructive heresies, even denying the sovereign Lord who brought them—bringing swift destruction on themselves.
> 2 PETER 2:1

My experiments prove that combining certain attractants, decoys, and calling techniques will tempt game animals to alter their normally cautious nature. Some animals will respond to even a single well-placed decoy. Others demand a more elaborate approach. To lure a trophy buck you may need several three-dimensional decoys, strategically placed, to create enough appeal. The effect, though, can be to make him become bold and proud, stomping his feet and snorting as he lets down his guard. His arrogance overrules his protective instincts and causes him to take risks that he would otherwise be too savvy to consider.

Aren't we sometimes like that foolish buck? Gullible to the wiles of the evil one, we let our pride, loneliness, weakness, or lack of information and spiritual grounding overrule our good sense. Today, scores of Christians are being misled by false prophets and cultic teachers. They should know better. But they are lured in by false promises, clever talk, and spiritual illusions, becoming susceptible to spiritual "decoys."

Christ warned His followers to beware of spiritual falsehood. "Watch out for false prophets," He said. "They come to you in sheep's clothing, but inwardly they are ferocious wolves" (Matthew 7:15). Like decoys, the deceivers of our time present themselves as gentle expounders of God's mind, but in fact they are raging wolves wanting to tear apart our sanity, our dignity, and our families. They cause us to disobey God's clear teachings and disregard our spiritual convictions. They expose us to grave dangers. If we sacrifice our convictions we will end up, like the unsuspecting buck, with the arrow of regret lodged in our side.

May God's wisdom overrule our gullibility and our prayer be as prudent as King Solomon's: "Keep falsehood and lies far from me" (Proverbs 30:8).

"FORGET-ME-NOTS" FOR FISHERMEN

A CHECK LIST OF TEN ITEMS NO FISHERMAN SHOULD LEAVE HOME WITHOUT.

Rod and Reel

Tackle Box

Sun Glasses

Hat

Net

Sun Screen

First Aid Kit

Bait

A Companion

Patience

"FORGET-ME-NOTS" FOR HUNTERS

A CHECK LIST OF TWELVE ITEMS FOR THE HUNTER'S DAY PACK.

Water

Energy Bars

Compass (GPS)

Knife

Rope

Whistle

Flashlight

First Aid Kit

Survey Tape for Marking Trail

Matches

Rain Parka

Solar Blanket

Anybody who fishes knows that
patience and perseverance
are keys to success.
The same holds true about our Christian walk.

AL LINDNER

BUCK FEVER

READ: GALATIANS 5:25

A very experienced hunter knows what I am talking about when I mention the term "buck fever." When the novice hunter has his first deer in his rifle sights, sometimes something just seems to snap. All reason and everything he has learned about hunting seems to momentarily flee his mind at the excitement of sighting his first buck.

Tom Rakow, founder and president of the Christian Deer Hunters Association, is considered by many to be a very good hunter, but he clearly remembers when he was first struck with buck fever.

Tom wanted to become a hunter even as a youth. For years he dreamed about the time when he could distinguish himself as a great outdoorsman by bagging his first deer. But to do that he had to have the opportunity to participate in a hunt. He was very excited, then, when on the first day of deer season one year, four friends invited him to come hunting with them. It was not long after leaving camp on the first morning of hunting that he had his first encounter with that nonfatal malady so common to first-time deer hunters.

"I will long remember the opening day of my very first deer season," explains Tom. "A member of our hunting party kicked out a nice six-pointer that stopped broadside only a few yards from me. You could not have asked for an easier shot. Unfortunately, I fell under the power of that dread disease, buck fever.

"I had heard that buck fever was famous for making hunters behave in some strange ways. It makes them do things like shout 'Bang! Bang!' and never fire a shot, or lever unfired rounds onto the ground. I even remember reading of one hunter who received two broken legs when he got so excited about shooting a large deer that he forgot he was sitting in a tree stand more than 15 feet off the ground when he ran to tag it!"

The effect of buck fever on Tom was to give him arms of lead. He knew what he wanted to do, but for some strange reason he just couldn't bring the rifle to his shoulder. Instead he shot eight times from the hip, hitting dirt and trees just a few feet from where he was standing. Tom recalls that the buck seemed to smile at him, winked, and darted back into the woods without a mark on him.

As powerfully debilitating as buck fever can be to the hunter, we struggle with a similar kind of fever in our Christian lives: sin. When we want to do the right thing, we often find ourselves stalled by the sin in our lives. This is a fever more powerful and more potentially devastating than any other. It is this that caused the apostle Paul to confess, "When I want to do good, evil is right there with me" (Romans 7:21). Sin constricts us from doing what we know we need to do.

Unlike the hapless hunter, though, we are not left alone to face the consequences of this fever. God has provided us a remedy to the power of sin in the person of the Holy Spirit. If we have truly trusted Jesus Christ as our Savior, the Holy Spirit dwells inside us and seeks to help us live lives that are pleasing to the Lord. As Paul reminded the believers in the young Roman church: "You, however, are controlled not by the sinful nature but by the Spirit, if the Spirit of God lives in you" (Romans 8:9). While there is no known cure for buck fever, it is good to know that there is a cure for sin.

Jesus Christ has given us the power of the Holy Spirit so that we need not fear the power and effects of sin. With His death on the cross He purchased our forgiveness. This is a truth that is very real for Tom Rakow. Although he missed the mark on his first hunt, he didn't miss the mark on the most important hunt of all—eternal and abundant life through Jesus Christ.

> The next day John saw Jesus coming toward him and said, "Look, the Lamb of God, who takes away the sin of the world!"
>
> JOHN 1:29

CAUGHT BY HIS OWN LURE

READ: 2 TIMOTHY 2:15

We all have embarrassing stories about fishing adventures—the time you fell into the lake fully clothed, the trip where you remembered everything except the bait, the day you capsized your boat through inattention to where you were going. No sportsman is immune from those embarrassing moments when things just don't seem to go the way you intend. Steve Chapman, author and singer/songwriter, has one of the most embarrassing stories I've heard. And it happened even before he got to the lake!

Steve was about 15 years old when a West Virginia gentleman invited him to go catfishing. Well, Steve jumped at the chance. Because the fishing hole was a long distance from his home, the man invited Steve to spend the night. That seemed a good idea, especially when he discovered that the man had a beautiful teenage daughter with long blond hair!

Steve's guest room was in the middle of the house, an area folks had to pass through on their way to breakfast in the morning. So when wake-up time came, Steve's modest nature dictated that he dress under the covers. He decided to hurry so that he would be ready before his new-found friend came by. He reached into his duffel bag and dug out his pants, wrestling them onto his bare legs. Next he reached for his sweater, intending to pull it on over his T-shirt. He felt around for it and when he had it in his hand he gave it a pull. It wouldn't come. Puzzled at the resistance he encountered in trying to remove it, he yanked harder and harder. It still wouldn't come. *One more hard pull should do it*, he thought to himself while reaching lower into the bag.

> I am not ashamed of the gospel, because it is the power of God for the salvation of everyone who believes: first for the Jew, then for the Gentile.
> ROMANS 1:16

With a sudden burst of pain he discovered what was tangling up the sweater. An artificial lure that he had brought from home had fallen out of its container and snagged his sweater. When he grasped for the sweater, the large rear treble hooks caught on the bag and the front ones drove into his thumb. "There was only one way to respond to the disaster," says Steve. "I screamed!"

In moments everyone within shouting distance arrived at the embarrassed boy's room, finding him hopping around with his bag and his sweater. The young girl and other family members tried to help, but they had a hard time restraining their laughter when they realized how difficult it would be to disconnect the boy from the lure, the sweater, and the bag. Though filled with sympathy, they couldn't ignore the humor of the situation.

After a visit to the medical center, Steve took his bruised ego fishing, where no one spared him from jests about the incident. In time, he was even able to laugh about it himself.

We have all been embarrassed at one time or another, feeling foolish about something we have said or done. Embarrassment is usually something we work hard to avoid. But if we make avoiding embarrassment the major goal of our lives, we will miss many great opportunities. For example, many people fail to testify to their faith in Jesus because they are afraid of feeling embarrassed. They are worried that they might not have all the right answers or that their own unworthiness may damage their testimony.

But Scripture tells us that we need to honor our relationship with Jesus by acknowledging Him in our thoughts, words, and deeds. We share what He has done for us, not because of our own strength and perfection, but because of His. We don't need to have all the answers. We don't need to be perfect. We don't need to be obnoxious or imposing. We just need to be available for the Lord to work through us and willing to share. If we fail to do this we will miss out on some of the richest blessings of this life and the next. Can you think of a cause more worthy of risking a little embarrassment?

A PHILOSOPHY OF ANGLING

"I FISH, THEREFORE I AM!"

In developing these philosophies, I am heavily indebted to those fishermen and philosophers who have inspired me: Patrick McManus, Jimmy Houston, Hank Parker, Al Lindner, and Homer Circle. Thanks for your encouragement!

The worse the fisherman, the better the philosopher.

Fishing is always better yesterday.

So many flies…so little time.

How much does a fish weigh? Depends who caught it!

You will always catch your biggest fish the day you leave your net and camera at home.

The greatest rate of growth for a fish is between the time you catch it and the time you first tell your friends about it.

Your tackle box will always open and spill just after you have organized it.

Smoked carp tastes just as good as smoked salmon when you ain't got no smoked salmon.

Two best times to fish are when it's raining and when it's not.

I fish, therefore I lie.

Anytime a man ain't fishin', he is frittering away his time.

It is the strict circumscription
of hunting and fishing—
those unwritten rules of ethics, etiquette, and propriety—
that define the challenge.

JIMMY CARTER

WHAT WINNING A TROPHY REQUIRES

READ: JAMES 5:8

I t took three trips to New Zealand, hours of climbing and glassing, a near-death experience with a helicopter, plus a whole lot of persistence before I finally got what I was after: a tahr. And not just any tahr, but one big enough to place in the top-ten-ever shot! It would have been easy to give up, to decide that it was too difficult trying to bag one of these elusive mountain goats. But I stuck with it, and the reward was one of the great hunting accomplishments of my life. Isn't that the way it usually is? The biggest achievements in life seldom come easily.

Many hunters pull themselves out of warm, comfortable beds and hike miles through overgrown trails in freezing weather so they can sit in a cramped tree stand next to a pond full of mosquitoes—all this for the mere possibility of seeing a trophy deer. Typically, these are the kinds of hunters who are most successful because they are willing to make the required sacrifices in order to experience the challenge of the hunt.

On His second ministry tour through Galilee, Jesus told His disciples the parable of the sower as a way of encouraging them to persevere. Explaining the parable He said, "The seed on good soil stands for those with a noble and good heart, who hear the word, retain it, and by persevering produce a crop" (Luke 8:15). Jesus was reminding His band of exhausted followers that to be spiritually effective they must persist and wholeheartedly dedicate themselves to the challenge.

Paul also reminds us that our identification with Christ is related to how we endure the task: "The things that mark an apostle—signs, wonders and miracles—were done among you with great perseverance" (2 Corinthians 12:12). Paul is suggesting that the mark of a great hunter of souls is determination.

Whether we are trying to tackle life's problems, provide leadership for others, or contribute to some great cause, our success depends upon our perseverance. The old phrase "hang in there, baby!" is more than an expression of encouragement. It is good advice for a disciple. As you persevere, you'll receive the rewards—even more thrilling than a world-record tahr!—that only patience can provide.

May the Lord direct
your hearts into
God's love and
Christ's perseverance.
2 THESSALONIANS 3:5

HUNG UP ON FISHING

READ: PSALM 30:5

E ven as a teenager, Hank Parker was hung up on fishing. He remembers a fishing trip to Lake Wylie, on the border of the Carolinas, where he literally got "hung up." It was an overcast afternoon in February, and fishing had been slow for the 17-year-old. He had spent most of the day carefully working a crankbait around some old submerged stumps at the mouth of a creek. As his deep-diving plug was biting into the muddy bottom, Hank suddenly felt a tug. Below the surface a fish quickly wrapped Hank's line around a root and refused to move. Hank bowed his back and mustered all his strength to pull his lure free. Suddenly the root broke, and the frustrated angler began to reel in his lure. He fully expected that the bass had long since freed itself from the snag and swum to safer waters.

When he lifted the tangle of dead limbs out of the water, however, Hank was surprised to find that the huge bass was still hooked! "I think the old fish was taking its last bite when he hit my lure," remembers Hank. "The crankbait looked like a crappie jig in his large mouth, and he wasn't fighting at all."

Many years later, Hank found himself "hung up" again. This time, it was at the World's Fair Fishing Tournament in Knoxville, Tennessee. He needed just one more fish to clinch

a victory when he hooked a monster, a beautiful eight- or nine-pound fish that could have won it all for him. Unfortunately, it got tangled up in a discarded trot line and some brush. He carefully maneuvered the boat over to the snag and began reeling. But as he reached down to grab the fish, the tangled bass slipped away from him. So did $50,000 in prize money.

Of course Hank felt a momentary flash of anger, but he didn't let it settle in. As a Christian, he understood that anger had no rightful place in his personality. Becoming angry accomplishes nothing and does nothing to change a situation. When we feel angry, we should turn this emotion over to God and let Him change our hearts. To remain angry is not to trust in Him.

We also need to be wise in deciding who we choose to spend time with, for the anger of others can rub off on us and rob us of spiritual blessings. As Solomon wisely taught, "Do not make friends with a hot-tempered man, do not associate with one easily angered" (Proverbs 22:24). How do you pick your friends? Are you hanging around with guys who are always blowing off steam or guys who have learned to deal with life's frustrations?

Frustrations are sure to come. Are you allowing yourself to become angry or learning to meet adversity with a righteous response?

> My dear brothers, take note of this: Everyone should be quick to listen, slow to speak and slow to become angry.
> JAMES 1:19

PHOTOGRAPHY CREDITS

Cover	Tim Christie		pp 64-65	Tim Christie
p 1	Tim Christie		p 66	Jim Grassi
pp 2-3	Tom Henry		p 67	Tim Christie
p 4	Jim Grassi		pp 68-69	Photodisk
p 5	Tim Christie		pp 70-71	Tim Christie
pp 6-7	Photodisk		pp 72-73	Tim Christie
p 8	Jim Grassi		p 75	Tim Christie
p 9	Jim Grassi		pp 76-77	Jim Grassi
p 10	Koechel Peterson		pp 78-79	Photodisk
pp 12-13	Photodisk		p 79	*Inset* – Koechel Peterson
p 13	*Inset* – Photogear		pp 80-81	Tom Henry
pp 14-15	Tom Henry		pp 82-83	Jim Grassi
pp 16-17	Tree Tops of Roturua		p 83	*Inset* – Koechel Peterson
p 18	Koechel Peterson		pp 84-85	Tim Christie
p 19	Tim Christie		pp 86-87	Photodisk
pp 20-21	Tom Henry		pp 88-89	Jim Grassi
p 22	Tim Chrsitie		pp 90-91	Tim Christie
p 25	*Arrows* – Jim Grassi		pp 92-93	Photogear
p 25	*Deer* – Tim Christie		p 95	Koechel Peterson
pp 26-27	Tree Tops of Roturua		pp 96-97	Tim Christie
pp 28-29	Tim Christie		p 98	Tim Christie
p 29	*Inset*–Jim Grassi		p 99	Koechel Peterson
pp 30-31	Tim Christie		p 100	*Inset* – Jim Grassi
pp 32-33	Tom Henry		pp 100-101	Photodisk
pp 34-35	Tim Christie		pp 102-103	Koechel Peterson
pp 36-37	Jim Grassi		p 104	Jim Grassi
pp 38-39	Koechel Peterson		p 105	Tree Tops of Roturua
pp 40-41	Photodisk		pp 106-107	Tim Christie
pp 42-43	Photodisk		p 108	Tim Christie
p 43	*Inset* – Tom Henry		p 109	Koechel Peterson
pp 44-45	Tim Christie		p 110	*Hunting* – Koechel Peterson
pp 46-47	Tim Christie			*Lab* – Jim Grassi
p 49	Tim Christie		pp 112-113	Jim Grassi
pp 50-51	Tim Christie		pp 114-115	Jim Grassi
pp 52-53	Photodisk		pp 116-117	Jim Grassi
pp 54-55	Charles Alsheimer		p 119	Koechel Peterson
pp 56-57	Tom Henry		pp 120-121	Jim Grassi
pp 58-59	Tom Henry		pp 122-123	Tim Christie
p 60	Jim Grassi		pp 124-125	Jim Grassi
p 62	Tim Christie		pp 126-127	Photodisk
p 63	Tom Henry			

FEEL FREE TO CONTACT AND SUPPORT THESE OUTDOOR MINISTRIES

CHRISTIAN BOWHUNTERS OF AMERICA
3460 West 13th St.
Cadillac, MI 49601
(616) 775-7744

CHRISTIAN DEER HUNTERS ASSOCIATION
P.O. Box 432
Silver Lake, MN 55381
(320) 327-2266

CHRISTIAN SPORTSMAN'S FELLOWSHIP
P.O. Box 566547
Atlanta, GA 31156
(800) 705-7892

FELLOWSHIP OF CHRISTIAN ANGLERS SOCIETY
P.O. Box 188
Cookson, OK 74427
(800) 213-6227

FISHERS OF MEN
3206 Thurber Rd.
Brooklyn Park, MN 55429
(612) 566-0638

GOD'S GREAT OUTDOORS
8193 Emerick Rd.
West Milton, OH 45383
(927) 698-3651

LET'S GO FISHING FAMILY MINISTRIES
P.O. Box 434
Moraga, CA 94556
(925) 376-8277

MY FATHER'S WORLD VIDEO MINISTRIES
43 Lima Rd.
Geneseo, NY 14454
(716) 243-5263